The Christian Family Christmas Book

EDITED BY

Ron & Lyn Klug

Augsburg Publishing House

Minneapolis

Library of Congress Cataloging-in-Publication Data

THE CHRISTIAN FAMILY CHRISTMAS BOOK.

Summary: Stories, poems, lore, prayers, and carols to celebrate the true meaning of Christmas.
1. Christmas—Literary collections. [1. Christmas—
Literary collections] I. Klug, Ron. II. Klug, Lyn.
PZ5.C462 1987 [Fic] 87-1391
ISBN 0-8066-2270-9

Manufactured in the U.S.A. 10-1113

1 2 3 4 5 6 7 8 9 0 1 2 3 4 5 6 7 8 9

Contents

Introduction 7
Stories and Poems

The Birth of Jesus 9
retold by Ron and Lyn Klug
A retelling of the biblical story of the Savior's birth.

Arizona Christmas 12
by Elizabeth Vollstadt
Kristi finds it hard to celebrate Christmas in her new home.

Jonathan's Gift 14
by Margaret Shauers
Jonathan has no money to buy Christmas gifts.

The ABCs of Christmas 16
A poem by Gloria A. Truitt

A Stranger on the Street 18
by Betty Lou Mell
Megan doesn't want to invite an Asian girl to her Christmas party.

The Magic Christmas Gift 20
by Frances Margaret Fox
Two young girls discover a special gift for their mother.

Christmas Carol 23
A poem by Sara Teasdale

The Loving Gift 24
by Gloria A. Truitt
Laura receives a special present from an elderly friend.

The Christmas Train 26
by Ivan Gantschev
When a landslide endangers a train, Malina has to act fast.

The Huron Carol 28
A poem by J. Edgar Middleton

Waiting for Christmas 29
by Margaret Springer
Amanda has a hard time waiting for Christmas.

Jeremy's Christmas 31
by Marjorie Ellert Berg
Jeremy doesn't want to spend Christmas at the senior-citizen's center.

What Can I Give Him? 34
A poem by Christina Rossetti

The Fir Tree 34
by Hans Christian Andersen
A family takes in the wandering Christ child.

What about Santa Claus? 36
by Ron and Lyn Klug
The history of St. Nicholas.

A Visit from St. Nicholas 38
A poem by Clement Moore

A Second Chance 41
by Hope Lind
After spoiling Greg's picture, Mary Ann is given a second chance.

Christmas Song 42
A poem by Eugene Field

David and the Doorstop 43
by Helen Mallmann
David can't get around to cleaning his room in time to go Christmas shopping.

Christmas through a Knothole 45
by Katherine Gibson
Even though Uncle Hans is in jail, Max and Gretchen help him celebrate Christmas.

Unexpected Guests 47
by Mabel N. McCaw
Stranded travelers make Christmas special for Susan.

Animals at the Manger 51
Four poems by Rudolf O. Wiemer, translated by Melva Rorem

The Jar of Rosemary 52
by Maud Lindsay
A young prince finds a way to gain a gift for his sick mother.

The Mysterious Christmas Gifts ..56
by Evelyn Wilharm
Ellie offers to baby-sit rather than go Christmas shopping.

Who Needs Jim? 58
by Margaret D. Woolington
What can Jim do to help the family prepare for Christmas?

Bobby's Presents 60
A poem by Elsie Duncan Yale

Legend of the Christmas Rose 61
retold by Ron and Lyn Klug
A shepherd girl finds a gift to offer the Christ child.

Tommy's Special Present 62
by Margaret Shauers
Tommy learns to appreciate the special gift from his grandmother.

Words from an Old Spanish Carol 64
A poem by Ruth Sawyer

Christmas on the Prairie 65
by Kit Lambeth
Amy is unhappy spending Christmas in a sod hut on the prairie.

Andy's Christmas Prayer 69
by Margaret Shauers
Andy prays for money to buy presents, and finds a 10-dollar bill.

Happy Oxen 70
A poem by Annette Wynne

Annelise and the Wooden Shoe ...71
retold by Ron and Lyn Klug
A German girl discovers a special Christmas gift.

Merry Christmas, Maria 74
by Mona K. Guldswog
A Mexican girl misses her family and their celebrations at Christmas.

Celebrating Christmas around the World 76
by Ron and Lyn Klug
Christmas customs in many lands.

Sing for Joy! 78
A psalm

Kurt Finds Christmas 78
by Nelda Johnson Liebig
Kurt discovers Christmas in an Eskimo village.

The Patchwork Skirt 80
by Alice Sullivan Finlay
Sally is sad because her mother is in the hospital at Christmas.

Until the Grass Sprouts 83
by Ron Matthies
George Henry is tired of winter!

The Wise May Bring Their Learning 85
A poem by Edward John Hopkins

R. R. Bear 85
by Marty Crisp
Sara has to spend Christmas in the hospital.

The Tree That Trimmed Itself 87
by Carolyn Sherwin Bailey
The Little Pine Tree wants to be a real
Christmas tree.

Company for Christmas 90
by Alan Cliburn
Jason finds a new friend at Christmas.

A Christmas Carol 93
A poem by Gilbert Keith Chesterton

How a Mouse Changed
Christmas 94
by Alice Cameron Bostrom
The story of how a little mouse led to the
composition of "Silent Night."

"For Hungry Poeple" 95
by Celia Lehman
Kristi and Teresa decide to give a Christmas gift
to hungry people.

The Practical Gift 97
by Phyliss Doudna
Bobby's flashlight turns out to be a practical gift.

Christmas Is Remembering 98
A poem by Elsie Binns

The Wooden Shoes of Little
Hans 99
retold by Ron and Lyn Klug
Little Hans befriends the Christ child and is
rewarded.

The Boy Who Hated Christmas .. 101
by Robert C. Gremmels
Tommy is jealous of his sister's presents.

Paul's After-Christmas Party 103
by Florence J. Johnson
Paul, whose birthday falls in January, plans a
special party.

Winds through the Olive Trees .. 106
A poem by Katherine Parker

A Bell Cookie 106
by Elizabeth Phillips
Nita doesn't want to give Ginger a Christmas
cookie.

In The Great Walled Country ... 108
by Raymond MacDonald Alden
Children learn it is better to seek gifts for others.

The Heart of Christmas 112
by Dr. Bernard M. Christensen
A wise Christian leader shares the true meaning
of Christmas.

Prayers

Thanks for Jesus 114
by Ron Klug

A Prayer 114
by Martin Luther

Prayer before Christmas 115
by Pat Corrick Hinton

Prayer at Christmas 115
by Pat Corrick Hinton

Prayer after Christmas 115
by Pat Corrick Hinton

Bless Us, Dear God 116
by Christopher Idle

A Christmas Prayer 116

O Lord Jesus 116

Thank You for Our Christmas
Tree 116
by Mildred Tengbom

We Remember Jesus 117
from M. H. Botting's collection

We're Happy at Christmas 117
by Ron and Lyn Klug

**Let Us Thank God for
Christmas** 117
by J. D. Searle

Christmas Prayer 118
by Robert Louis Stevenson

Dear Baby Jesus 118
by Margaret Kitson

I'm So Excited! 118
by Chris Jones

Carols

The Friendly Beasts 119
Away in a Manger 120
Pat-a-Pan 120
Mary Had a Baby 121
**Hush, My Babe, Lie Still and
Slumber** 122
**I Am So Glad Each Christmas
Eve** 122
Go Tell It on the Mountain 123
**Rise Up, Shepherd, and
Follow** 124
O Little Town of Bethlehem 125
We Three Kings of Orient Are .. 126

Acknowledgments

Acknowledgments 127

Introduction

Christmas. A season of love. A time to share the joy with children. A holiday rich in meaning as we celebrate the birth of the Savior. But how do we share the true meaning of Christmas with our children and grandchildren? How do we communicate the love of God revealed in the coming of the Christ child?

One simple way is by taking a child onto your lap and reading a Christmas story or poem, singing a carol together, or saying a Christmas prayer. Fewer activities create a warmer relationship than reading aloud, and stories are a wonderful way to transmit Christian values to children.

To help you share the meaning of Christmas with the children you love, we have gathered together this *Christian Family Christmas Book*. It contains 40 stories for reading aloud, beginning with a retelling of the story of Jesus' birth as we find it in the pages of the New Testament. The other stories, written by many different writers, have been chosen to explore the many joys and problems of a family's celebration of Christmas. Included are a few articles that explain some Christmas customs. And some of the stories are just for fun.

All the stories can be read to preschoolers and children in the early elementary grades. By second and third grade many children will be able to read the stories for themselves.

We have also chosen some fine poems about Christmas, a collection of prayers, and some carols especially appropriate to sing with younger children.

As in our earlier anthology, *The Christian Family Bedtime Reading Book,* we suggest that you may want to try a simple family reading ritual. Begin with a story or two. If your child indicates that he or she wants to discuss the story, do so. But don't try too hard to teach a lesson; let the story itself do that. Just enjoy the story together. Then follow with a poem, sing a carol or two, and end with a prayer.

You could begin such a ritual during the busy days of preparing for Christmas, taking a few minutes out to relax together and focus on the meaning of the coming holiday. Continue throughout the Christmas season, which traditionally lasts until January 6. (Of course, we can reflect on the meaning of Christmas at any time of year.) Through such a simple family time together, you and your children can grow in love for one another and for the Lord, whose birth we celebrate at Christmas. This is our prayer for you.

The Birth of Jesus Retold by Ron and Lyn Klug

Many many years ago, God's people were waiting. They had been waiting a long time for the Savior God had promised to send.

In the city of Nazareth there lived a young woman named Mary. She was not yet married, but had promised Joseph the carpenter that she would become his wife. Mary loved God and believed that some day God would send the Savior.

Then one day something very special happened to Mary. An angel appeared to her. "God is with you," the angel said. "You will have a son, and you will call him Jesus. He will be great and will be called the Son of God."

Mary was filled with joy when she heard the angel's words. She said, "I am God's servant. I will do whatever God wants."

Soon after that, God spoke to Joseph in a dream. "I want you to take Mary as your wife," God said. "She will have a baby who will be God's Son. You will call him Jesus, because he will be the Savior of the whole world."

When Joseph woke up, he remembered his dream and he married Mary, as God had told him.

The emperor, a powerful ruler across the sea, decided to count all the people in his kingdom. He did this so he would know how much taxes people would pay and how many soldiers he would have for his army. He ordered everyone to go back to their hometowns to be registered.

This meant that Mary and Joseph had to travel from Nazareth to Bethlehem. It was a long, hard journey, especially for Mary, who would soon have her baby.

It was late in the day when Mary and Joseph arrived in Bethlehem. They were tired and hungry, but the village was so crowded that all the hotels and inns were full. Mary and Joseph could find no place to stay. *What will we do?* Mary wondered. *Where will the baby be born?*

Finally, one kind innkeeper felt sorry for Mary and Joseph. "There is no room in our inn," he said. "But you may stay in my stable with the animals."

There in the stable Mary and Joseph slept among the oxen and donkeys. And there in the quiet of the night Jesus was born.

Mary wrapped him in clean cloths to keep him warm. Joseph put some clean hay in the manger to make a soft bed for the baby Jesus.

In the hills around Bethlehem shepherds were guarding their sheep. Suddenly a bright light filled the sky. An angel appeared, and the shepherds were frightened.

"Don't be afraid," said the angel. "I bring you good news, news that will bring joy to all people. Tonight in Bethlehem the Savior is born. This is how

you will know him: you will find him wrapped in cloths and lying in a manger."

Suddenly the sky was filled with angels who sang, "Glory to God, and peace to God's people on earth." Then, as suddenly as they had appeared, the angels were gone.

The shepherds said to one another, "Let's hurry to Bethlehem and find the baby." So they ran to Bethlehem and found the baby Jesus as the angel had said. They knelt down and worshiped him. Then they returned to their sheep, praising God and telling everyone they met the good news about Jesus.

When Jesus was a week old, Mary and Joseph took him to the temple in Jerusalem. There they thanked God for the gift of a child.

An old man named Simeon was there. He took the baby Jesus in his arms and said, "Lord, you have kept your promise and sent the Savior. He will be a light for the whole world."

In the temple there was also an old woman named Anna. When she saw Jesus, she told everyone she knew that the baby was God's Son.

Far away in a distant land, some Wise Men searched the sky. One night they saw a bright, new star. In those days people believed that a special star meant that a new king had been born. So the Wise Men set out to find the new king.

For many days they traveled through strange lands, following the star. Because they were looking for a new king, they stopped at the palace in Jerusalem. There they asked King Herod, "Where is the new king who has been born?"

Herod was worried. *A new king? What are these strangers talking about?* he wondered.

He called for some of his oldest men, who told him, "The ancient scrolls say that a new king will be born in Bethlehem."

Herod told the Wise Men, "Go to Bethlehem and find the new king. Then come back and tell me so I can go and worship him too." But what Herod really wanted to do was kill the little boy so he could not grow up to be king.

The Wise Men left the palace, and again the special star shone in the sky. It led them to the house where Mary and Joseph were now living. There, the Wise Men knelt and offered Jesus gifts—gold, frankincense, and myrrh.

When it was time for the Wise Men to leave, God told them, "Don't go back to Herod, because he wants to kill the baby." So they returned to their own land another way.

When King Herod learned that the Wise Men had fooled him, he was angry. He ordered his men to kill all the babies in Bethlehem. God told Joseph in a dream, "You are in danger. Take Mary and Jesus and hurry to the land of Egypt. Stay there until I tell you to come back."

Mary and Joseph dressed quickly, bundled up Jesus, and left Bethlehem as soon as they could. They traveled all the way to Egypt, where they lived until it was safe for them to return home.

Back home in Nazareth, Jesus lived happily with Mary and Joseph.

When Jesus grew up, he taught people God's Word. He healed sick people and fed those who were hungry. He died and rose again to become our Savior and King. Each year at Christmas we celebrate Jesus' birthday and thank God for the gift of his Son.

Arizona Christmas

Elizabeth Vollstadt

Kristi's brown eyes glared at the blue sky outside. The radio announcer had just given the temperature: 80° Now he continued, "While we enjoy beautiful weather this Christmas Eve here in Desert Springs, Arizona, the East is preparing for a big snowstorm. At least eight inches are expected by midnight in most of New England and—"

Kristi didn't wait to hear the rest. Eyes filled with tears, she turned off the radio and flung herself on her bed. How she hated it here! It was bad enough that they had to move, but to do it right before Christmas just wasn't fair.

She closed her eyes and pretended she was in the white colonial house near Boston where she had spent the first 11 years of her life. *Maybe when I open my eyes, this will all be a bad dream,* she thought. When her younger brother Jeff burst into the room, however, she opened her eyes to sunshine instead of snow, Arizona instead of New England.

"Come on outside," Jeff said. "Dad's bought some lights to put on the house. He says this is the first year he doesn't have to worry about freezing his hands off. Then we're going to string some around the big saguaro cactus on the front lawn."

"What lawn?" asked Kristi. "There's no grass around here, just brown earth with a few clumps of cactus. Big deal!"

Jeff looked disgusted. "You know what I mean," he said. "Besides, I think the cactus garden is nice. Dad says a lot of them flower in the spring. You can stay here if you want to. I just came in because dad suggested it."

On his way out, he flung over his shoulder, "I don't know why he cares about you anyway. All you're doing is ruining everybody's Christmas."

No, I'm not, thought Kristi. *Mom and dad ruined it when they decided to move.* Still, Jeff's words hung in the air, and Kristi wondered if maybe she was being unfair.

Her parents had tried to explain the move to her, tried to make her understand. Dad had been very unhappy with his selling job. Here he was in research, something he had always wanted to do.

12

"Of course, it's going to be hard on all of us for a while," her mother had said. "But the important thing is that we'll all be together."

The smell of molasses cookies and the sound of Christmas carols drifted through the doorway. For as long as Kristi could remember, she and Jeff and mom had always baked molasses cookies the afternoon before Christmas, just as mom had always done with grandma and Aunt Betty when she was a girl. She felt bad leaving mom to do it alone. Maybe she would help. Then the radio in the kitchen began playing "Winter Wonderland." Kristi was reminded of the snow at home and the desert outside. Instead of joining her mother, she shut the bedroom door.

Through the open window, she saw Jeff and her father putting the last of the lights on the saguaro cactus. Its thick, prickly arms were laced with wires.

"Turn on the lights, dad," yelled Jeff. The sun was shining so brightly Kristi couldn't see that it made any difference whether they were on or not.

"How does it look?" her father called, seeing her face at the window.

"It looks dumb," Kristi answered, "just like everything else around here."

No one came near her until it was time for supper. Then, while she ate in stony silence, her parents and Jeff talked about the Christmas Eve service they were going to in a little while.

"This is the only night of the year when the church is lit entirely with candles," her mother said.

"The Michaelsons next door told us that people come from all over, even if they don't belong to the church," added her father.

Dusk was slowly approaching when they left the house. By the time they reached the church, its white, stone walls glowed pink in the sun's last rays.

Inside, it was almost dark. A few men were quietly lighting candles in the wrought-iron chandeliers hanging over the altar. They threw light on a simple wooden crèche in a garden of red poinsettias.

Kristi's parents stood uncertainly in the back of the church. Then they saw the Michaelsons waving them over. "Merry Christmas," all the adults said to each other, shaking hands. Jeff and the two Michaelson boys nodded shyly at each other. Kristi pretended she was invisible.

Suddenly, a hush came over the congregation as a white-robed children's choir started up the center aisle. They were singing "Silent Night," their faces lit by the single candle each one carried. The singing swelled as the congregation joined in.

Kristi remained silent, but soon the familiar words of peace and love and joy began to work their magic. A few minutes later she was singing her favorite carol, "Joy to the World," along with everyone else. When she reached, "Let e-e-v'ry-y hea-a-rt pre-pa-are hi-im ro-o-om," however, the words stuck in her throat like a piece of hard candy.

Why, she hadn't been preparing room for him at all. Her heart was so full of resentment, there wasn't room for anything else—not her parents, not Jeff, not Jesus. The door was shut, just as her bedroom door had been shut all afternoon.

Feeling ashamed, she squeezed her mother's arm and looked up at her. "I'm sorry I didn't help you with the cookies this afternoon."

Her mother smiled. "I know," she answered, putting her arm around Kristi's shoulder. "I left a few for you to decorate, just in case."

Kristi's father leaned over to give her a kiss. "Merry Christmas, sweetheart," he said. "Welcome home."

Kristi kissed him back. Home. New England would always be a part of her. She knew that, but maybe Arizona could be home, too, if she gave it a chance.

She looked at the Christ child lying in the candlelit crib. "Merry Christmas," she whispered. There was room for him now.

Jonathan's Gift

Margaret Shauers

*I*t was a cold morning. Jonathan's nose and cheeks turned red as he walked down the sidewalk. But Jonathan hardly noticed the cold. He felt too sad. In one more day it would be Christmas, and Jonathan had no presents to give his friends.

I wish I was old enough to have a paper route like my sister Janice, thought Jonathan. *She bought presents for all her friends.*

Jonathan stopped in front of Mrs. Ridges' house. Mrs. Ridges was a good friend. Every year she baked a beautiful cake for Jonathan's birthday.

Even if I can't buy Mrs. Ridges a present, I should wish her a Merry Christmas, he decided, and walked to her door.

"Jonathan!" she said when she saw him, "I'd hoped you would visit today. I baked a big Christmas cookie for you. You may take it home and eat it after lunch."

Jonathan took the cookie. He smiled and said, "Thank you." But he felt worse than ever because he had no present for her.

"I wanted to give you a present," he said, "but I didn't have any money."

"Why, Jonathan!" exclaimed his friend, "you've given me a present already, by coming to see me today. My son can't come home this Christmas. If it weren't for you, my Christmas would have been very lonely."

"I'm glad I came," said Jonathan. "I don't want you to feel lonely." Then he smiled. He would ask mother to invite Mrs. Ridges for Christmas dinner. Mother wouldn't want her to spend Christmas Day alone. And, since he would be the one to tell mother, it would really be a Christmas present to Mrs. Ridges from him.

I wonder if my other friends think my visits are Christmas presents, Jonathan thought when he was walking down the street again. Then he shook his head. Mr. Brown wouldn't!

No one understood why Jonathan liked Mr. Brown. Mr. Brown was old like Mrs. Ridges, but he wasn't nearly as nice.

I don't know why I do like Mr. Brown, thought Jonathan as he shuffled through the thin covering of snow on Mr. Brown's walk. *He never says good things about anyone. But he carves such beautiful little animals from wood. I like to see the animals, I guess. Besides, Mr. Brown is sick and can hardly walk. That might make anyone crabby.*

When Jonathan knocked at his door, Mr. Brown said, "Oh, it's you again." When Jonathan went inside, he said, "There, boy! You stay on that rug, or you'll track snow all over the house. I can't scrub the floor just because you were foolish enough to come out in the snow." Then he asked, "What's that you're holding?"

"A Christmas cookie," answered Jonathan. "I'm telling all my friends 'Merry Christmas' this morning. Mrs. Ridges gave me this cookie."

"Hrmph!" snorted Mr. Brown. "That silly old woman's going to make you sick with her sweets." Then he reached into the big box where he kept the carved animals.

"Here," he said, pushing a brown shape at Jonathan. "At least this won't give you a belly-ache!"

Jonathan stared at the little animal in surprise. He had watched Mr. Brown carve this horse, and even Mr. Brown had been pleased because it was so pretty.

"Are you sure you want me to have it?" Jonathan asked.

"Of course I'm sure," snapped the old man. "I may be old and crippled, but I know what I'm doing! Now you get along home. Your overboots are dripping on the rug!"

Jonathan's boots weren't dripping at all. But he just smiled and said, "Thank you, Mr. Brown. Merry Christmas!" Then he went outside and felt surprised all over again.

Mr. Brown must like him after all. This was the best animal he'd ever carved! Jonathan smiled. He knew something he could do for Mr. Brown, too.

Jonathan put his cookie and the beautiful horse on a newspaper that lay on Mr. Brown's front porch. Then he ran around the house and found an old broom in the garage.

The snow wasn't nearly so deep as Mr. Brown thought. Soon Jonathan had the walk swept clean.

Now Mr. Brown won't need to worry about anyone tracking snow on his floor, he thought. *And once I tell people about this horse, everyone will know that Mr. Brown isn't as crabby as he sounds. Then they might come to tell him "Merry Christmas" too.*

Jonathan had more friends to visit. But now he was smiling as he walked down the sidewalk. There would be something special he could do for everyone. And he didn't need money for the gift of friendship he wanted to give.

The ABCs of Christmas

Gloria A. Truitt

Advent is a special word
　Beginning with an **A.**
It means a time of waiting, and
　It ends on Christmas Day.

Bethlehem begins with **B**
　And there our Lord was born
In a manger long ago
　On that first Christmas morn.

C stands for the Christ child who
  Brought peace to all on earth,
And **D** is for December when
  We celebrate his birth.

E stands for the Eastern star
  That led the shepherds to
That humble stable where they learned
  The angels' words were true.

Frankincense begins with **F.**
  This gift was one of three
The Magi brought to introduce
  The first epiphany.

G is for almighty God
  Who sent his only Son,
That we may have eternal life—
  Each and everyone!

Holly starts with **H** and is
  A festive greenery,
And **I** is for the icicles
  Upon the Christmas tree.

They called him Jesus, Son of God—
  His name begins with **J,**
And truly he is King of kings
  Which starts with letter **K.**

L is for his lasting love—
  He's with us everyday—
And **M** is for the manger where
  He slept upon the hay.

N is for the word, Noel,
  Which means a Christmas carol.
O for ornaments that dress
  Your tree in gay apparel.

P is for poinsettias
  That bloom at Christmas time,
For postmen bringing presents that
  Are tightly bound with twine.

Q is for the quiet peace
  Encompassing the earth

Every Christmas Eve when we
  Recall the Christ child's birth.

The letter, **R,** and letter, **S,**
  Stand for radiant star,
A guiding light for worshipers
  Who traveled from afar.

T is for the tinsel and
  The tolling of church bells,
For trimming trees and tasty treats
  And tummy-tempting smells.

U is for unending, like
  Our wishes of good cheer,
Because the Christmas spirit lives
  Within our hearts all year.

While Mary watched and kept him safe,
  The baby Jesus slept,
So **V** is for the vigil that
  His mother, Mary, kept.

Wreath begins with **W.**
  This holiday decor
Welcomes yuletide visitors
  Who knock upon your door.

The ancient Greeks wrote **X** for Christ—
  Now, Xmas is a word
That some folks write for Christmas, but
  It's one that's rarely heard.

Y is for the Yule log with
  Its fire warm and bright
That ushers in each Christmas Eve,
  A blessed, holy night.

Z is for the zealous faith
  That Christians 'round the earth
Have in Christ, and that is why
  We celebrate his birth!

Though Christmas is a sacred time,
  And comes but once a year,
May all our days be filled with love
  And tidings of good cheer!

A Stranger on the Street Betty Lou Mell

I'm glad we decided to bake Christmas cookies early, mom," Megan said. "It makes the house cozy warm."

"I think so, too. We'd better put them away though," her mother replied as she pulled another cookie sheet from the oven. "If they're out when your father and Jeff get home, they'll be gone before Christmas."

Megan smiled. "We'll put some in tin cans for friends and neighbors, right?" she asked.

"Speaking of neighbors," her mother reminded her, "have you invited our new neighbor to your 'make a gift' party?"

Megan frowned. "I meant to yesterday, but I got busy in school and didn't get around to it."

"Don't wait too long," her mother said as she slid another cookie sheet into the oven. "Your party's only two weeks away."

Megan scooped the chopped nuts into a measuring cup. "Here's the last of the nuts," she said. Then she brushed the crumbs from the cutting board. "Mom—"

"What, honey?"

"Wo Chin is Asian. She probably doesn't even know what Christmas is about."

Her mother chuckled. "Maybe—but *you* know what Christmas means!"

"But she wouldn't feel comfortable with the other kids."

"You'd make her feel comfortable," her mother encouraged her. "Looks like we are going to need more nuts."

Megan jumped up quickly. "I'll run down to the store and buy some. Give me a minute to bundle up."

"Take $10.00 out of my wallet and get a big bag!" her mother called.

Megan shielded her face against the wind as she trudged through the snow. At the gate she turned left and followed the snow-covered hedges along the street. Ahead, the lights of Petrack's store glowed brightly.

Megan stopped at the curb, looked both ways, then stepped forward. Instantly, she felt herself slipping. Her gloved hand broke her fall, but her knee stung sharply.

Suddenly, someone was behind her, helping her up. "Are you all right?" a caring voice asked.

Megan felt like a klutz. "I think so. I didn't know the street was so slippery," she replied, looking over her shoulder at a teenage boy. "Thanks!" She struggled to keep her balance and brush the snow from her coat.

"If you are going to the store, I will help you across," he offered.

Megan nodded and grabbed the hand he offered. Carefully, he led her step by step, and when they reached the store, he opened the door for Megan to enter first. Once inside, he hurried to the back of the store while she got the bag of nuts. When Megan got to the counter, the boy was there with a can of vegetables. He glanced at her and smiled as he counted his money.

Megan looked closer—he was Asian! *I wonder if he is Wo Chin's brother?* she thought.

"Getting colder," Mrs. Petrack said as she slipped the nuts into a grocery bag. "Tell your mother I'll soon have those candied fruits she wanted."

Megan took the change and smiled. She dropped the change into her glove and slipped it over her hand. "Thanks, Mrs. Petrack," she called as she left the store.

The boy waited outside, shuffling his feet and looking at the icy street. "My name is Wo Tom. I waited to help you across again," he said. "I live at the end of the block."

"I'm Megan Cook," she replied as she clutched the bag and held his hand. "Are you related to Wo Chin?"

"I'm her brother."

As they reached the other side of the street, Wo Tom said, "There, made it safely." He quickly walked away.

"Thanks!" Megan called happily.

He waved over his shoulder. "Be careful!" he called.

Megan pounded onto her porch and tapped her boots against the top step.

Then she glanced up the street. She could see Wo Tom's outline against the snow as he walked. She lifted her chin happily and went inside. "Mom, I fell on the ice," she said as she put the nuts on the table. Megan went into the bathroom, rolled up her pant leg, and propped her foot on the side of the bathtub. "It's just a tiny cut."

"I'll put antiseptic and a bandage on it," her mother said, opening the medicine cabinet.

Megan watched her mother as she smoothed the adhesive strips of the bandage. "You're right, mom," she said.

Her mother chuckled. "Oh, what about?"

"I kept thinking about how different Wo Chin and her family are," Megan said. "But Christmas means the same thing for everyone—no matter how we look or talk. God loves us all the same."

Her mother nodded. "You're right. But—now where are you going?" she called as Megan raced into the kitchen.

"To find out Wo Chin's phone number from the operator. I have to invite her to my party! We need a lot of help making those gifts for the children's hospital!"

The Magic Christmas Gift

Frances Margaret Fox

*I*t was late autumn in the north woods, and Beatrice and Josephine were thinking about Christmas. They liked to think about Christmas; they liked to talk about it and to sing Christmas songs and to play Christmas games. Those two little girls had been known to play the game of Santa Claus filling Christmas stockings on the Fourth of July, and it was such fun they did not care who laughed.

Beatrice was seven years old and Josephine was nine that particular autumn day when they climbed to the top of the front gate posts to talk it over. There was no gate in front of

their log cabin, only an opening where a gate would some day swing on hinges and fasten with a click. The gate posts were made of big, round logs of cedar, and were almost two feet taller than the top of the fence. There was a path leading from the gateway to the front door of the log cabin, and behind the cabin, and surrounding it on three sides, were the evergreen woods. In front of the cabin was a wide clearing belonging to the railway.

From early spring until late in the autumn the little girls were in the habit of climbing on the gate posts to watch the trains go by.

"I suppose if we had lots of money," said Beatrice from the top of her gate post, "I suppose we could go to Marquette and buy Christmas presents for the whole family!"

"But most of all for mother!" added Josephine, happily kicking her feet.

"What should we get mother if we had money and could go traveling?" Beatrice inquired.

"Well," answered Josephine, "if we ever have a ride on the cars, and if we ever go to Marquette with father and our pockets full of money, we'd buy— we'd buy—I don't know what and you don't know what!"

At that, the two little girls laughed and laughed until they almost fell off the gate posts; they liked to sit on the gate posts and laugh. For a while they talked about the Christmas presents they should like to make.

"But there should be something special for our mother," insisted Josephine.

"Oh," answered Beatrice, as she happily kicked her feet against her gate post, "I guess we'll have to give mother the same old promise we give her every Christmas, that she will have all the year two little girls, oh, such good little girls, to help take care of babies and tidy up the cabin, tra la-la, tra la-la-la!"

After that, until the afternoon train whistled, the merry little girls kept choosing gifts for all the family, but most of all for mother. But the minute the train whistled, Beatrice suggested a new game.

"When the train starts puff-puff from the station just round the curve over there," said she, "and the wheels begin to turn round slowly, and the cars come slowly, rumble-rumble, you turn square round facing the train this way, just like me, and you sing with me this song I am just thinking up, and we'll try Christmas magic, like this:

"White magic,
Christmas magic,
Send our mother
a Christmas gift!

"Gold magic,
Christmas magic,
Send our mother
a Christmas gift!"

By the time the passenger train was opposite the little log cabin, the laughing children were gazing straight toward it, singing over and over to the rumble of the wheels:

"White magic,
Christmas magic,

Send our mother
a Christmas gift!

"Gold magic,
Christmas magic,
Send our mother
a Christmas gift!"

Of course those two little girls away off in the upper peninsula of Michigan, miles and miles from any town, did not expect a magic Christmas gift for their mother; they simply had a good time, and forgot all about their game as soon as it was over and they had climbed down from their gate posts to go to the pasture after the cows.

But the day before Christmas, when the little cabin was bursting with Christmas joy and secrets, the postmaster from the settlement called to see Beatrice and Josephine. He said he wished to speak with them alone. There was only one room in the cabin, one big, clean, cheerful room, and so the little girls climbed into the postmaster's sleigh and drove with him beyond sight of the house. Then he said "Whoa!" to his horses, and without another word he untied a big, flat parcel that looked like a picture in a frame; and it was a picture in a frame—a big picture of two merry-looking little girls, each seated on a gate post in front of a log-cabin home that had evergreen woods behind it and a clearing in front.

It was a long time before either child could speak; then Josephine whispered, "How did it happen?"

"A lady on a passing train who is a stranger to us all," the postmaster answered, "took a snapshot of you two, because you looked so happy. Then she had the picture enlarged and framed and sent it to me to give to you, so that you might give it to your mother for Christmas. She said she was sure I would know who you were by the picture; so, as I thought you would like a big Christmas surprise for your mother, I asked to see you alone. Now we'll drive back to the house."

At last Beatrice found her voice, but "Did you ever!" was all she said, and "Did you ever!" was all Josephine said, until they remembered to thank the postmaster for his kindness.

On Christmas Eve the little girls could keep their secret no longer, and solemnly presented their mother with the magic gift.

Mother cried. Tears of joy rolled down her face when she saw it.

"I never before had a picture of any of you children," said she, "and I never expected to, because we live so far from a photographer. And this is so beautiful! Such happy faces! Oh, it seems too good to be true! It would not have happened if you were not such good little girls, always thinking of your mother!"

The next day two joyous little girls danced about the cabin, singing:

"White magic,
Christmas magic,

Brought our mother
a Christmas gift!

"Gold magic,
Christmas magic,
Brought our mother
a Christmas gift!"

And the two little faces in the picture smiled down upon the happy family cheerfully, then and ever after.

Christmas Carol

Sara Teasdale

The Kings they came from out the South,
    All dressed in ermine fine;
They bore him gold and chrysophrase,
    And gifts of precious wine.

The Shepherds came from out the North,
    Their coats were brown and old:
They brought him little new-born lambs—
    They had not any gold.

The Wise Men came from out the East,
    And they were wrapped in white:
The star that led them all the way
    Did glorify the night.

The Angels came from heaven high,
    And they were clad with wings:
And lo they brought a joyful song
    The host of heaven sings.

The Kings they knocked upon the door,
    The Wise Men entered in,
The Shepherds followed after them
    To hear the song begin.

The Angels sang through all the night
    Until the rising sun,
But little Jesus fell asleep
    Before the song was done.

The Loving Gift

Gloria A. Truitt

Mother watched Laura carry the box of freshly baked cookies across the street to Mrs. Gilly's door. She turned to give her mother a brave smile, and then pressed the doorbell. Laura wished her stomach would stop doing flip-flops. She had not wanted to deliver the cookies because she had never talked with Mrs. Gilly. She was afraid she wouldn't know what to say. Soon the door opened and Laura disappeared into Mrs. Gilly's front hall.

An hour later, Laura's mother looked at the kitchen clock. It was suppertime and Laura still wasn't home. When she heard Laura's father coming home she decided not to wait any longer. Just as she picked up the phone to call, Laura ran into the house. "Mother! Mother!" Laura called excitedly. "I had the best time with Mrs. Gilly! You should see her doll collection!"

During supper, Laura told her mother and father about Mrs. Gilly. "Mrs. Gilly told me all about her life," said Laura. "It was such an exciting story, I forgot about the time."

"I understand," said mother. "Will you tell us about her dolls?"

"Oh, they're just wonderful," sighed Laura. "Mrs. Gilly is 86 years old, and some of the dolls are almost as old as she is! She keeps them on shelves in a big, glass case, and there's a story about each one of them!"

At bedtime, Laura asked her mother if she could visit Mrs. Gilly again. "She's very old," said Laura thoughtfully, "and I think she's lonely."

Time passed and Laura's visits to Mrs. Gilly became quite regular. Three afternoons a week she stopped by to chat with her new-found friend, and each time she came home with an interesting story to tell her mother.

Laura told mother about the lovely doll with the China head, and a very strange doll that was made from corncob. "The oldest doll still wears its original dress!" exclaimed Laura. "It was made by Mrs. Gilly's mother—and it doesn't have a single tear in it—can you imagine that?"

Mother smiled and said, "I'm sure they are all beautiful, Laura, and I'm glad Mrs. Gilly has time to tell you about them."

"You know, mother, they *are* all beautiful, but the most beautiful doll of all is not very big—or old, compared to the rest. It's a black-haired doll with a pink gown and matching hat. Mrs. Gilly's sister made the doll, and gave it to her on her 65th birthday!"

One Saturday morning, Laura woke up to find the ground covered with snow. She bounced out of bed when she remembered that this was the day her father had promised to get their Christmas tree. After breakfast the family went to the tree farm where they inspected hundreds of trees. Finally they decided on a beautiful Norway spruce. As her father tied it to the top of the car, Laura slowly walked over to a small, but perfectly shaped balsam fir. "Oh,

please, could we get this one for Mrs. Gilly?" called Laura. "It would be just perfect for her!"

"That's a wonderful idea," said father.

When the family arrived home, mother and father helped Laura carry the tree to Mrs. Gilly's house. When Mrs. Gilly saw the pretty balsam fir, her eyes filled with tears of happiness. "How can I thank you?" she asked, hugging Laura tightly.

"You don't have to," answered Laura, "you're my friend—and this is a special time for love."

"You're right, Laura," said Mrs. Gilly, "Christmas is the time to celebrate the *greatest* gift of love—the birth of Jesus."

After they had visited for a while, mother said it was time to go. Just as Laura was going out through the door, Mrs. Gilly said, "Wait a minute, Laura. I almost forgot to give you something." Quickly, Mrs. Gilly picked up a brown paper bag from the table and tucked it under Laura's arm. "It's a small gift," said Mrs. Gilly, "but I'd like you to have it as a keepsake."

At once Laura knew what was in the bag because the tiny doll in the pink gown was no longer standing in the glass case. Laura hugged Mrs. Gilly and said "Thank you" over and over again. Then everyone laughed happily as Laura took the little doll from the bag and cried, "This isn't a small gift, Mrs. Gilly! It—it's the biggest love gift I've ever had! Thank you, thank you, thank you!"

The Christmas Train

Ivan Gantschev
translated by Stephen Corrin

Many years ago in a little railway station in Switzerland there lived a signalman named Wassil and his small daughter, Malina.

The railway track ran through many tunnels and was hemmed in by steep hills. It was part of Wassil's job to keep an eye on those dangerous stretches of the line.

One afternoon, the day before Christmas Eve, Wassil was checking the track while Malina was busy decorating the Christmas tree with the little stars she had made herself. She was eagerly looking forward to the present her father had promised to bring her.

Suddenly she heard a frightening rumble; it sounded like thunder. Her dog, Belo, began to bark and scratch at the door. "It's the sound of falling rocks," cried Malina, and she rushed outside, frightened out of her wits. Indeed, there, right in the middle of the track, lay an enormous boulder. Malina felt quite helpless. What on earth was she to do? "The express will be here in half an hour. What would daddy do? I must warn the engine-driver!" All sorts of thoughts flashed through her mind as she ran back indoors.

"Light a fire 400 meters ahead of the spot where the accident happens and swing a lamp"—that's what her father had always told her to do if an emergency like this occurred.

Without further ado she picked up the Christmas tree, not bothering about the decorations, and snatched the big railwayman's lamp off its hook. Then she ran as fast as her legs could carry her. There was barely a quarter of an hour left. By the light of the lamp she stumbled, panting, through a tunnel, then out again, hurrying between the rails till she got to a second tunnel. She could now hear the sound of the approaching train.

Hastily, with trembling hands, she set fire to the Christmas tree with the matches which she luckily hadn't forgotten to bring with her. Just at that very moment the express came thundering furiously from out of the black hole of the tunnel. The engine-driver shrank back with terror at the sight before his eyes. What he saw was a bright fire and a small child swinging a large red lamp. Immediately he slammed down the emergency brake and shut off the steam-regulator. The whistle shrieked. The great train shuddered and came grinding and gasping to a gradual halt.

In the luxury restaurant-car everything flew wildly up and down again in tremendous confusion. The fish landed in the soup, the cream cakes went flying into the passengers' faces, and the tablecloths wrapped themselves round the waiters. What a how-d'you-do!

Huffing and puffing, the giant locomotive had stopped just in front of Malina. The engine-driver and guard jumped out and rushed up to the little girl. The driver recognized her at once. "It's Malina!" he exclaimed. "What happened?"

"Down there, right in front of this next tunnel, a huge lump of rock has fallen down. I had to stop your train," explained Malina breathlessly to the two startled men.

Meantime the news of the rock fall had traveled like wildfire through the train and soon everybody knew that little Malina had saved their lives.

"The child must be half frozen," someone said. They took Malina by the hand and led her into the cozy warm dining-car.

A lot of mysterious whispering seemed to be going on among the passengers. Suddenly Malina found herself showered with presents. And then—her father appeared in the doorway! Cradled in his arms was a tiny lambkin—snow-white with black spots behind his ears. She ran up to him. This, she knew for sure, was her Christmas present.

"Come on, daddy," Malina said, all excited, "let's go home. Belo must be waiting for us."

To show how grateful he was, the engine-driver gave them a Christmas tree which he had freshly dug up from the station siding. So now they could celebrate Christmas properly after all.

And where, you may ask, did I hear this story? It's quite simple. Once I spent Christmas in that little railway-station—with my aunt Malina and my grandfather, the signalman, Wassil.

The Huron Carol

J. Edgar Middleton

'Twas in the moon of winter-time,
When all the birds had fled,
That mighty Gitchi Manitou*
Sent angel choirs instead;
Before their light the stars grew dim,
And wandering hunters heard the hymn:
  Jesus your King is born.

Within a lodge of broken bark
The tender Babe was found,
A ragged robe of rabbit skin
Enwrapped his beauty round;
But as the hunter braves drew nigh,
The angel-song rang loud and high:
  Jesus your King is born.

The earliest moon of winter-time
Is not so round and fair
As was the ring of glory on
The helpless Infant there.
The chiefs from far before him knelt
With gifts of fox and beaver-pelt.
  Jesus your King is born.

O children of the forest free,
O sons of Manitou,
The Holy Child of earth and heaven
Is born today for you.
Come kneel before the radiant Boy,
Who brings you beauty, peace and joy.
  Jesus your King is born.

*Gitchi Manitou: the supreme God

Waiting for Christmas

Margaret Springer

Amanda hopped on one foot and then on the other. "This is fun," she said, "Being a string of lights in the Christmas play. Not many kids get to be that."

"No," said Amanda's mom, sewing. "And not many moms get to make the costume. It isn't easy turning you into a string of Christmas lights, Amanda."

"Can I help you, mom? Can I help you?" Amanda pushed a chair next to the sewing machine.

"You can give me pins," said her mother. "That will speed me up."

Amanda climbed on the chair and reached for the pins. She knocked the scissors and pattern onto the floor. She picked them up, and knocked the pins over.

"Amanda," said her mother, "I think it will be better if I sew by myself. After you pick everything up, get your crayons and make a Christmas picture."

It was easy making a Christmas picture. The whole house smelled of Christmas cookies, and snowflakes were drifting down outside. If only it weren't so long to wait!

Amanda made 10 Christmas pictures. She made more than 10. She had to get more paper. Her mother was busy sewing.

"Look at my pictures, mom! Look at my pictures!"

Her mother looked. "Those are lovely, Amanda," she said. "We'll put them up on the fridge and—oh, Amanda! Look what you colored on!"

"What?"

"You used the backs of my posters for the choir concert!"

"I thought it was scrap paper," said Amanda.

"It wasn't scrap paper," said her mom. She sighed. "Amanda, I have an idea. Will you sit here and tidy my sewing box for me?"

Amanda liked that job. She put away needles and thread. She sorted buttons. She rolled up measuring tapes. And while she did, she sang Christmas songs. Finally she closed the sewing box. But she kept something interesting in her hand.

Amanda went to the bathroom and shut the door. She opened her hand and looked at the blue, plastic case with the tiny scissors inside. She had never seen such tiny scissors before. "I wonder if they can really cut?" she whispered.

She looked at herself in the mirror, and held a little chunk of hair away from her round face. "I'll just try them out," she whispered. "No one will notice."

"Amanda," her mother called after a while. "I need you to try this on."

Amanda went.

"Oh, *Amanda!* What on earth have you done to your hair?"

"I just trimmed it a little," said Amanda.

Amanda's mom put her head in her hands. Then she tried to smile. "Amanda," she said, "sit right there on the floor and think about what you did. And promise me you will never, ever, do that again."

"OK, mom," said Amanda sadly. She sat right there on the floor and wondered why waiting for Christmas was so much trouble.

After a while Amanda's mother got some scrap paper. "Now I'll show you a fun thing to do with scissors," she said. She folded the paper over and over until it was small. Then she cut out fancy shapes, and opened it out again.

"A snowflake!" said Amanda.

"Yes," said her mother. "Now you make snowflakes while I finish these sleeves."

Amanda made snowflakes. She made big snowflakes and little snowflakes. She used up all the paper. "Can I make more, mom?"

"Sure. Use the scrap paper that's on the desk."

Amanda made more snowflakes. "I'm making a pretty blue one for you, mom," she said.

"That's nice, Amanda." Her mother put away the sewing things. "Now, we've just got time to take you to the hairdresser and get to the bank before it closes. Where's the paycheck daddy left out for me?"

"Was it blue?" asked Amanda, looking at the back of her blue snowflake.

"Oh, *Amanda!*" said her mom.

Amanda's mom went to the phone to call Amanda's dad. She did not say anything when she came back.

They picked up all the pieces of snowflake paycheck they could find. Then they went out. Amanda pulled her woolly hat low over her hair and ears. Still her mother did not say anything.

It was snowing softly. Amanda looked up at the snowflake patterns in the sky. She looked down at the snowflake patterns on the sleeve of her snowsuit.

"I'm sorry, mom," she said quietly.

"That's OK, Amanda," said her mother, putting an arm around her. "Tomorrow will be a better day."

The hairdresser gave Amanda a new, short haircut. The bank people cashed the snowflake paycheck. Amanda and her mother put up choir posters all over town.

That night Amanda was ready for bed early. The play was tomorrow.

"Are you ready to be tucked in, Amanda?" called her mother.

But Amanda was already fast asleep. She was dreaming of posters and plays, and sewing and snowflakes, and Christmas songs and haircuts. And in her dreams, while she waited for Christmas, she didn't get into any trouble at all.

Jeremy's Christmas   Marjorie Ellert Berg

Jeremy pressed his nose against the bedroom window. He had hoped there would be a snowstorm today. Then he wouldn't have to go.

"Jeremy, it's time to get dressed," dad called. "We have to be at the Senior Center in an hour."

Jeremy tugged off his pajamas. He wished they were going to Aunt Liz's instead. She would make lots of food, and he could play with his cousins. Christmas was supposed to be spent with your family, not feeding people you don't even know.

Jeremy was pulling on his socks when he heard his father call, "Time to go. Get your coat on, and lock the door on your way out. I'm going out to start the car."

Jeremy slowly finished getting dressed. He was taking his coat off the hook when his father came back in.

"The car won't start," he complained. "I'll try it again in 10 minutes."

"Dad, do we have to go?" Jeremy asked.

"Jeremy, we've been blessed this year. I have a better job, and we bought this house. Now I want to do something for someone else."

When his father went out to try the car again, Jeremy hoped it wouldn't start. He didn't want to watch other people enjoying their dinners while he worked.

Before long, Jeremy's father rushed into the house. "Let's go. I finally got the car started."

Zipping up his jacket, Jeremy trudged out the door, slamming it shut. He sat quietly as they drove to the Senior Center. He could tell this was going to be an awful Christmas!

The aroma of roasting turkey, baking ham, and fresh rolls made Jeremy hungry as soon as he walked in the door of the Senior Center. But he couldn't eat until later. And he would be eating leftovers—on Christmas.

Jeremy spent the next hour putting napkins, knives, forks, and spoons on the long tables in the dining room. His dad went to pick up people in the Senior Center van. As the people came in, they smiled at the gaily decorated dining room. A few walked in slowly and looked sad.

As he was walking to the kitchen, Jeremy saw his father coming toward him with a tiny, wrinkled lady leaning on his arm. Her coat was worn and thin. Jeremy wondered how she stayed warm in the cold weather.

"Jeremy, this is Mrs. James," his father said. "Will you help her with her coat?"

"Just find me a place to sit," Mrs. James grumbled. "I don't know why they made me come today."

As Jeremy found an empty chair for Mrs. James, he thought, *Why do I have to spend my Christmas helping such a grouch?*

When everyone had finished eating, Jeremy cleared the tables. As he carried away dirty dishes, he noticed that people were sitting very quietly. Some looked tired. Others just stared into space.

After a short worship service, Jeremy's father led singing of Christmas carols. Then he asked if anyone could remember a special Christmas. Jeremy glanced around the quiet room.

Finally a woman with braids coiled around the back of her head began, "One year our Sunday school sang carols at the hospital. You should have seen those sick people smile." Jeremy watched the dimples in her round face deepen as she recalled the carols she had sung.

"When I was 10, I built a bookshelf for my mother," said a man sitting across from Jeremy. Jeremy listened as the bent-over man spoke. Lights reflected from a bald spot on the top of the man's head. "My mother kept that shelf for years even though it was so crooked the books leaned."

After the man finished, Jeremy whispered, "I made a tie rack with crooked pegs for my dad. He hangs his favorite ties on it."

Jeremy and the man both smiled.

"I remember cutting down a Christmas tree for our house," said another person.

Jeremy recognized the voice of grumpy Mrs. James. Only now she didn't sound so grouchy.

"After my father broke his arm, my sister and I knew it was up to us. We grabbed a saw and headed for the woods." Mrs. James's eyes sparkled as she described the tree cutting. For the first time she smiled.

Jeremy grinned as he pictured tiny Mrs. James struggling with a dull saw and dragging a tree across icy snow drifts.

"That tree was so crooked, we couldn't get it to stand straight, no matter how we tried. It leaned so much, we finally tied a cord from a curtain rod so it wouldn't tip over." She laughed as she told the story. Soon the whole room was filled with laughter.

Now people no longer hesitated to speak. Many shared a memory of a long-ago Christmas.

When it was time to leave, Jeremy noticed Mrs. James heading for the coat rack. He hurried over to help her with her coat.

After fastening the last button, Mrs. James grabbed Jeremy's hand. "Thank you so much. This is the best Christmas I've had in years. And you helped make it that way."

Jeremy could see a tear slip down her cheek. He put his arms around Mrs. James and hugged her.

Later, as they walked to the car, Jeremy asked his father, "Dad, can we do this again next year?"

What Can I Give Him?

Christina Rossetti

What can I give him,
Poor as I am?
If I were a shepherd
I would bring a lamb,
If I were a Wise Man
I would do my part—
Yet what can I give him?
Give my heart.

The Fir Tree

Hans Christian Andersen

Most children have seen a Christmas tree, and many know that the pretty and pleasant custom of hanging gifts on its boughs comes from Germany; but perhaps few have heard or read the story that is told to little German children, respecting the origin of this custom. The story is called "The Little Stranger," and runs thus:

In a small cottage on the borders of a forest lived a poor laborer, who gained a scanty living by cutting wood. He had a wife and two children who helped him in his work. The boy's name was Valentine, and the girl was called Mary. They were obedient, good children, and a great comfort to their parents. One winter evening, this happy little family was sitting quietly round the hearth, the snow and the wind raging outside, while they ate their supper of dry bread, when a gentle tap was heard on the window, and a childish voice cried from without, "Oh, let me in, pray! I am a poor child, with nothing to eat, and no home to go to, and I shall die of cold and hunger unless you let me in."

Valentine and Mary jumped up from the table and ran to open the door, saying, "Come in, poor little child! We have not much to give you, but whatever we have we will share with you."

The stranger-child came in and warmed his frozen hands and feet at the fire, and the children gave him the best they had to eat, saying, "You must be tired, too, poor child! Lie down on our bed; we can sleep on the bench for one night."

Then said the little stranger-child, "Thank God for all your kindness to me!"

So they took their little guest into their sleeping-room, laid him on the bed, covered him over, and said to each other, "How thankful we ought to be! We have warm rooms and a cozy bed, while this poor child has only heaven for his roof and the cold earth for his sleeping-place."

When their father and mother went to bed, Mary and Valentine lay quite contentedly on the bench near the fire, saying, before they fell asleep, "The stranger-child will be so happy tonight in his warm bed!"

These kind children had not slept many hours before Mary awoke, and softly whispered to her brother, "Valentine, dear, wake, and listen to the sweet music under the window."

Then Valentine rubbed his eyes and listened. It was sweet music indeed, and sounded like beautiful voices singing to the tones of a harp:

"Oh holy Child,
   we greet thee! bringing
Sweet strains of harp
   to aid our singing.
"Thou, holy Child, in peace
   art sleeping,
While we our watch without
   are keeping.
"Blest be the house wherein
   thou liest,
Happiest on earth, to heaven
   the nighest."

The children listened, while a solemn joy filled their hearts; then they stepped softly to the window to see who might be without.

In the east was a streak of rosy dawn, and in its light they saw a

group of children standing before the house, clothed in silver garments, holding golden harps in their hands. Amazed at this sight, the children were still gazing out of the window, when a light tap caused them to turn around. There stood the stranger-child before them, clad in a golden dress, with a gleaming radiance round his curling hair. "I am the little Christ child," he said, "who wanders through the world bringing peace and happiness to good children. You took me in and cared for me when you thought me a poor child, and now you shall have my blessing for what you have done."

A fir tree grew near the house; and from this he broke a twig, which he planted in the ground, saying, "This twig shall become a tree, and shall bring forth fruit year by year for you."

No sooner had he done this than he vanished, and with him the little choir of angels. But the fir-branch grew and became a Christmas tree, and on its branches hung golden apples and silver nuts every Christmastide.

Such is the story told to German children concerning their beautiful Christmas trees, though we know that the real little Christ child can never be wandering, cold and homeless, again in our world, inasmuch as he is safe in heaven by his Father's side; yet we may gather from this story the same truth which the Bible plainly tells us— that anyone who helps a Christian child in distress, it will be counted unto him as if he had indeed done it unto Christ himself. "Inasmuch as ye have done it unto the least of these, my brethren, ye have done it unto me."

What about Santa Claus?

Ron and Lyn Klug

The story of Santa Claus is many, many years old. It begins with a man named Saint Nicholas. He was a real person, as real as you or I. He lived a long time ago, about 300 years after Jesus was born. Saint Nicholas lived in the land we now call Turkey. There he was a bishop, a great Christian leader. Some people say that Nicholas became a bishop when he was hardly more than a boy.

Saint Nicholas was very kind and generous. He loved to give gifts, especially to children. According to one story, there was a poor nobleman who had three daughters. Because he did not have enough money, his daughters could not get married. Saint Nicholas felt sorry for them and wanted to help, but he wished to do it secretly.

So one night he went to the nobleman's house, climbed on the roof, and threw a little bag of gold down the chimney. It landed in a stocking that had been hung by the fireplace to dry.

The next night Saint Nicholas threw another bag of gold down the chimney, and it landed in another stocking.

The third night the nobleman waited up to see who was being so generous. As he watched, Saint Nicholas dropped a third bag of gold into another stocking. And so Saint Nicholas was found out.

Some say that because of this story, people hang stockings by the fireplace at Christmas. An orange in the toe of the stocking can remind us of the bag of gold Saint Nicholas gave.

Because Saint Nicholas was so kind and generous, people remembered him and told stories about him. Hundreds of years later, children celebrated his feast on December 6.

Because Saint Nicholas had become a bishop when he was very young, school boys elected a "boy bishop," who dressed in splendid robes and led a parade through the streets.

Even today, in Germany and some other countries, children hang stockings on December 6 for Saint Nicholas Day, and find them filled with fruit and nuts and candy.

In Holland the Dutch children called Saint Nicholas *Sinter Klaas*. On Christmas Eve the children put their wooden shoes in front of the fireplace. They hoped that *Sinter Klaas* would leave gifts in the shoes. The children also put out hay for the saint's horse.

The Dutch who came to America brought the story of *Sinter Klaas* with them. When American children tried to say *Sinter Klaas*, it came out as "Santa Claus," and that's what we call him today.

About the same time the name of Saint Nicholas was changed to Santa Claus, his appearance also changed. Before this, Saint Nicholas was pictured as a tall, dignified man wearing a bishop's hat and robe, and sometimes riding a horse. In 1809, a famous American writer, Washington Irving, described Santa Claus as a typical Dutch settler in New York at the time. His Santa Claus was a fat, jolly man wearing large Dutch britches and a broad-brimmed hat, and smoking a long pipe. He rode above the trees in a wagon and dropped presents down the chimneys.

In 1822, a man named Clement Moore wrote a poem about Saint Nicholas, the one that begins, " 'Twas the night before Christmas. . . ." He gave Saint Nicholas a sled pulled by eight reindeer, and even provided the deer with names: Dasher, Dancer, Prancer, Vixen, Comet, Cupid, Donder, and Blitzen. He pictured Saint Nick, dressed all in fur from his head to his toe, as a jolly old elf with a fat belly that shook when he laughed.

A few years later an American cartoonist, Thomas Nast, drew a series of pictures showing Santa Claus making toys in his workshop and leaving the toys in stockings hung by the fireplace. This is Santa Claus much as we know him today.

In different countries Santa Claus is called Saint Nicholas, *Sinter Klaas*, *Pere Noel*, the *Weinachtsmann*, Father Christmas, or Kris Kringle. What-ever he is called, Santa Claus is always one who finds joy in giving to others.

As we have seen, Santa Claus is based on a real person—Saint Nicholas, who believed in Jesus and who enjoyed giving gifts. Over hundreds of years people made up stories about Saint Nicholas and drew different pictures of him, until today he is like the Santa Claus we see on television and in books and in shopping centers.

Santa Claus is not the most important thing about Christmas. The most important person is Jesus, whose birthday we celebrate. But when we see Santa Claus, we can remember the kind man named Saint Nicholas. When we think about Santa Claus bringing gifts, we can remember that all good gifts come from God—and the best gift God gave was Jesus, who came to show us God's love.

A Visit from St. Nicholas

Clement Moore

'Twas the night before Christmas,
when all through the house
Not a creature was stirring,
not even a mouse;

The stockings were hung
by the chimney with care,
In hopes that St. Nicholas
soon would be there;

The children were nestled
all snug in their beds,
While visions of sugarplums
danced in their heads;

And Mamma in her 'kerchief,
and I in my cap,
Had just settled our brains
for a long winter's nap;

When out on the lawn
there arose such a clatter,
I sprang from the bed
to see what was the matter.

Away to the window
I flew like a flash,
Tore open the shutters
and threw up the sash.

The moon on the breast
of the new-fallen snow,
Gave a lustre of midday
to objects below,

When, what to my wondering
eyes should appear,
But a miniature sleigh,
and eight tiny reindeer,

With a little old driver,
so lively and quick,
I knew in a moment
it must be St. Nick.

More rapid than eagles
his coursers they came,
And he whistled, and shouted,
and called them by name;

"Now, Dasher! Now, Dancer!
Now, Prancer and Vixen!

On, Comet! On, Cupid!
On, Donder and Blitzen!

"To the top of the porch!
To the top of the wall!
Now dash away! Dash away!
Dash away all!"

As dry leaves that before
the wild hurricane fly,
When they meet with an obstacle,
mount to the sky;

So up to the housetop
the coursers they flew,
With a sleigh full of toys,
and St. Nicholas too.

And then in a twinkling,
I heard on the roof,
The prancing and pawing
of each little hoof—

As I drew in my head,
and was turning around,
Down the chimney St. Nicholas
came with a bound.

He was dressed all in fur,
from his head to his foot,
And his clothes were all tarnished
with ashes and soot;

A bundle of toys
he had flung on his back,
and he looked like a pedlar
just opening his pack.

His eyes—how they twinkled!
His dimples, how merry!
His cheeks were like roses,
his nose like a cherry!

His droll little mouth
was drawn up like a bow,
And the beard of his chin
was as white as the snow;

The stump of his pipe
he held tight in his teeth,
And the smoke it encircled
his head like a wreath;

He had a broad face
and a little round belly,
That shook when he laughed,
like a bowlful of jelly.

He was chubby and plump,
a right jolly old elf,
And I laughed when I saw him,
in spite of myself,

A wink of his eye
and a twist of his head,
Soon gave me to know
I had nothing to dread;

He spoke not a word,
but went straight to his work,
And filled all the stockings;
then turned with a jerk,

And laying his finger
aside of his nose,
And giving a nod,
up the chimney he rose;

He sprang to his sleigh,
to his team gave a whistle,
And away they all flew
like the down of a thistle.

But I heard him exclaim,
ere he drove out of sight,
"Happy Christmas to all.
And to all a good night."

A Second Chance

Hope Lind

*I*n Sunday school this morning you may make a picture of the part of the Christmas story you like best," said Miss Louise.

Mary Ann thought about the baby in the manger. She thought about the angels and the shepherds. She thought of a starry night and of the special star that led the Wise Men. The sky must have been a big blue blanket splattered with stars. That's it! She would make a picture all of stars.

Her box of crayons lay beside her clean white sheet of paper. She took yellow and red, her favorite colors, and began making stars. Big ones and little ones. Thin ones and fat ones. It was fun, but her picture didn't look as nice as she had thought it would.

Across the table Greg was making his picture. Mary Ann stopped making stars to watch him. He had made a brown camel with two big humps. A man on top was holding the reins to the camel's head. In the sky was one big star with every point a different color.

Greg looked up from his picture at Mary Ann. "I like this big star I made," he said.

Mary Ann thought his picture was nicer than hers. A hard, angry feeling came up to her throat. "I don't," she said crossly.

She grabbed her pencil and made big scribbles over Greg's star. Greg looked at her in surprise. His brown eyes got wet. Mary Ann felt uncomfortable.

She saw Miss Louise watching her. Miss Louise looked sad. Mary Ann began to be sorry herself. She had been unkind, she knew.

"That's too bad, Greg," said Miss Louise. "You had such a bright star for the camel and Wise Man to follow. Would you like a clean piece of paper to make another picture?"

Greg nodded his head and brushed his sweater sleeve across his eyes. He took the clean paper and began making another camel.

"Mary Ann," said Miss Louise, "I gave Greg a second chance to make a picture. Would you like a second chance at something, too?"

In a small voice Mary Ann said, "What?"

"Would you like a second chance to be kind?" Miss Louise asked. She didn't seem angry. Mary Ann had the feeling that Miss Louise wanted to help her be kind.

"Yes," Mary Ann said.

"Fine," Miss Louise smiled and gently put her hand on Mary Ann's head. Then she went around the table looking at the pictures other children were making.

Mary Ann watched Greg make his new picture. It seemed even nicer than the first one.

A second chance to be kind, Miss Louise had said. How could she be kind now? Maybe she could think of something nice to say.

When Greg put his crayons away, Mary Ann told him, "Your picture is pretty."

Greg smiled proudly. "I think so, too," he said.

Suddenly Mary Ann didn't feel hard and angry inside. Her happiness was like the rising sun getting bigger. On her paper she quickly added one big orange star, to be the special star, and a yellow sliver of a moon. Her picture pleased her better now. In her mind she could still see a big blue blanket splattered with stars. She felt that a second chance to be kind gave her a second chance at her own picture.

Mary Ann hummed a happy hum. How good to have second chances!

Christmas Song

Eugene Field

Why do bells for Christmas ring?
Why do little children sing?

Once a lovely shining star,
Seen by shepherds from afar,
Gently moved until its light
Made a manger's cradle bright.

There a darling baby lay,
Pillowed soft upon the hay;
And its mother sang and smiled,
"This is Christ, the holy Child!"

Therefore bells for Christmas ring,
Therefore little children sing.

David and the Doorstop

Helen Mallmann

How does my stuff get all over the place?" David mumbled to himself as he looked around his messy room.

Just then his sister, Louise, appeared at the door. "David! *When* are you going to clean your room?" she asked.

"I don't know," David answered, wishing she'd go away so he could plan his next project.

"You've got so much junk!" said Louise. "Why are you saving all those rocks and cardboard boxes and pieces of wood and shells and the TV cart the neighbors put out for the trash pickup? You ought to throw that junk away!"

"Someday I might need it to build something," said David, still thinking about his project.

"Remember what mom said. Your room has to be all straightened up before you can go shopping. Dad will be home at 3:00, and the stores close at 5:00, because this is the day before Christmas. It's your *last* chance to get Aunt Julie's Christmas present."

"Yeah, I know," muttered David as he sat down on the only bare spot on the floor.

"Wait until I tell mom!" said Louise, and she stomped off down the hall.

Louise found her mother downstairs in the den.

"Mom, David will *never* get his room cleaned up by the time dad gets home. He's just sitting there in the middle of that mess. You're not going to take him anyway, are you?"

"David knows his room has to be cleaned up or he can't come shopping with us," answered mother.

"But he doesn't have a present for Aunt Julie."

"Well, that's *his* problem," replied mother.

Louise took two steps at a time up the stairs and stopped at her brother's bedroom door. "David, you haven't done a *thing* to straighten up this room! Look at your bed! It's covered with dirty clothes, blocks, books, your baseball and bat and mitt, and your dump truck! Why is a *dump truck* on your bed, anyway?"

"There wasn't room anywhere else, I guess," David said with a sigh.

Louise reached over and lifted the toybox lid. "It's empty! Why don't you put your toys in it? You'd better get going! Dad will be home any minute!"

"Yeah, I know," replied David softly.

The dog barked. The front door opened and closed.

"I bet that's dad! He's home and we're *leaving*," Louise muttered.

Mother came upstairs and stopped at David's bedroom door. She looked around the room.

He looked up at her and took a deep breath.

"David, the bargain we made yesterday was, you clean up your room and we'll take you shopping. I hope you can explain this to Aunt Julie. We'll be back about 5:00. Good-bye."

"Bye," said David.

At last the house was quiet, and he knew what he wanted to make. He reached for a flat piece of wood, two large smooth rocks, and his glue. Working quickly but carefully, he glued and painted and set the project

aside to dry.

When he heard voices in the kitchen, he put his project into a box, carried it carefully down the stairs, and stood in the doorway, waiting.

"David, what have you got there?" his dad asked.

"It's a doorstop for Aunt Julie," David replied.

"Great, David!" said his dad. "Show us how it works!"

"Aunt Julie will slide the middle part under the end of the door like this," he said as he showed them, using the kitchen door. "The two rocks at the ends will keep the door from blowing open or slamming shut."

"I like the pictures you painted on the rocks," said mother. "I'll get some wrapping paper."

Louise helped David wrap the gift, and he set it under the Christmas tree in the living room.

After supper David went up to his room and read a book. Later he smelled popcorn and went down to the kitchen.

"Louise," Dad was saying, "would you like to read the story of the first Christmas tomorrow, from your Bible storybook?"

"Sure, dad, I'll do that. What's David going to do?"

"David, will you play 'Silent Night'? I'm certain grandma and Aunt Julie would like to hear you play the piano tomorrow."

"OK," David said with a sigh. He stuffed his mouth with popcorn.

This Christmas Eve it was David's turn to place the Christ child in the nativity scene under the tree. After saying good night to mom and dad, the children climbed the stairs.

"David, it was nice of you to make that doorstop for Aunt Julie. But now you've *got* to clear the stuff off your bed so you can sleep in it," said Louise as she went to her bedroom.

"I suppose so," said David.

A little later David heard voices in the hall. His parents had come upstairs to bed, too.

He sighed. As he looked around the room, he made himself a promise, "I'll do it first thing in the morning before company gets here. It'll be an extra Christmas surprise for mom because she didn't get mad about the mess."

He took off his shoes, pulled his sleeping bag down from the closet shelf, and slowly tiptoed downstairs. After lifting the cat off the living room sofa, he spread out his sleeping bag, crawled in, and fell asleep.

Christmas through a Knothole

Katherine Gibson

Old Hans was the best wood-carver in all the land. But just three weeks before Christmas, he was thrown into jail! Again and again he had been told not to hunt in the king's own hunting ground. But Hans's mouth would water for the taste of roast rabbit, and to the king's lands he would go and set his traps. This time, alas, Hans was caught.

The jailer was a kind man. Since Hans was old, he let him have a fire and some wood to carve. But Hans was very unhappy. To be in jail on Christmas, when all the village was making merry!

Hans lived all alone, but he had a good friend named Gretchen. Gretchen was seven years old and had big gray eyes and long, smooth, yellow hair in two pigtails. Gretchen also had a little brother named Max. He was as round and brown as she was pink and white. He was as naughty and full of laughter as she was quiet and thoughtful.

"Oh, Max," Gretchen said to her brother, "what shall we do? Poor Uncle Hans is in jail, just for hunting rabbits. He always has his Christmas dinner with us. Now he won't have any—not a bite."

"And worse than that," said Max, "we won't get any toys!" For every year, of course, Old Hans carved the most wonderful toys for them.

Max looked cross. Gretchen looked sad. They walked past the jail. Like all the other houses in the village, it was made of wood. The walls were very thick, and the only window was far, far above their heads.

Suddenly Max said, "Look, there is a hole."

It was a large knothole in the wood. Max stood on his tiptoes and put his eye to the hole. "I can see him. I can see Old Hans. He is carving, just the way he always does!"

"Oh, Max, let me see!" cried Gretchen. She bent down, and sure enough she could see Old Hans—or part of him.

Max took out his pocket knife (every boy in the village carried a knife) and scratched at the hole until he made it bigger. Then he put his lips to the hole and called. "Hans, Uncle Hans, come here! Come to the knothole!"

Old Hans was surprised. He got up and followed the sound of the excited small voice. The children told him all the village news. In turn, he told them how long the days were in jail.

"It will be a sad Christmas for you, Uncle Hans," said Gretchen. "We will miss you at home."

"For us it will be even worse." Max was almost crying. "We won't have any toys—not one!"

"You come back here tomorrow," Uncle Hans said.

The children could hardly wait for the next day. In the morning, they hurried back to the knothole. "Here we are, here we are, Uncle Hans," they shouted.

The knothole was bigger now. Out of it, Uncle Hans pushed a tiny wooden figure. It was a little boy carrying a flower in his hand.

"Oh," cried Max, "it is just like me!"

"Only you never carry flowers," said Gretchen. "You just carry big sticks."

The next day, a fat duck came through the knothole. Then a market woman. "Why," said Gretchen, "that is old Martha!"

Day after day, the tiny carved figures came through the knothole. At last the children had a whole village. And not one toy was more than three inches high.

"Uncle Hans has done so much for us," said Gretchen. "I wonder, can we make him a knothole Christmas dinner?"

They talked with their mother. And this is what they did. They wrapped some fine pieces of roast goose into long, thin bundles, four of them. They took some long, thin sausages that Hans liked ever so much. Gretchen baked some rolls. They were a very funny shape, not very different from the sausages, long and thin. Even the Christmas cakes were rolled up tight, with sugar and nuts inside.

"And a tall, thin candle—a Christmas candle. I will make it myself," said Max. And he did.

Christmas Eve came. There was snow on the pointed roofs of the houses, and on the pointed tops of the fir trees. Just as the lights were lit, Max and Gretchen went to the jail.

They called Old Hans. He came and gave them the prettiest toy of all. It was a funny, fat, little fellow with a star on his head—a Christmas angel. Then Max pushed, and Gretchen pushed, and soon Hans's Christmas dinner was inside the jail. Last of all, Max pushed through the candle.

"Made it myself!" he said proudly, jumping up and down.

The children said they had never had such toys, never. And they loved them because they were so tiny. And Hans said the best dinner he ever had was the Christmas dinner through a knothole.

Unexpected Guests

Mabel N. McCaw

*I*t was Christmas Eve. Susan Harper stood staring out the front window. The snow was still falling, adding to the drifts on either side of their driveway.

"Cheer up, sis," said her 10-year-old brother Matt from his chair near the radio. "There's no need to ruin Christmas just because the snowstorm makes it impossible for us to go to grandma's."

"But we don't even have a tree," wailed Susan. "And we didn't make any Christmas cookies, because grandma said she was taking care of that."

"Guess we can get along without a tree," said Matt. "And there's still time to make cookies."

Just then an announcement over the radio caught Matt's attention.

"Pardon this interruption," the announcer was saying, "but there are several families who have been brought into the city from their stranded cars on the highway. Perhaps there are some families here who would like to take them into their homes for Christmas. If so, call 555-6751 and we will be glad to put you in touch with your unexpected guests. Remember, the number to call is 555-6751."

"555-6751," Matt repeated and then dashed into the kitchen.

"Hey, mom," he called. "Did you hear that? Some families have been stranded by the storm. Let's invite one of them to spend Christmas with us."

Just then a car drove into their driveway, and Susan came bounding into the kitchen.

"He got one! He got one!" she cried, running to open the door for her father.

"Got what?" Matt asked.

But Susan didn't have to answer because her father came in dragging a Christmas tree behind him.

"For our stranded family!" Matt exclaimed. "We can have a family for Christmas, can't we? All we have to do is call 555-6751 and they'll tell us where we can find the family."

"Merry Christmas!" called Mr. Harper as he shook the snow from his hat and shoulders. "What's this about a stranded family?"

Matt told his father about the radio announcement. "Please, dad, let's have one of the families come here. I'll let them have my room. I can sleep on the daybed in the playroom."

"Well, what do you say, mom?" Mr. Harper asked. "And what does Susan think about the idea?"

"Let's do it!" Susan called from the storage closet where she was already getting out the decorations for the tree. "Having visitors would be fun."

"I guess that's it, then," said Mr. Harper. "Unless you think it will be too much work for you."

"Bringing happiness to others at a time like this will be worth it," Mrs. Harper replied.

"And I'll help!" Susan called.

"Then let's call." Mr. Harper phoned the station and received the name of a family with a boy and girl about the ages of Matt and Susan, and a four-month old baby.

While Mr. Harper went to pick up the family, Susan and Matt helped their mother get ready. They put clean linen on Matt's bed and fixed up a large clothes basket as a bed for the baby.

"The girl can sleep in the other bed in my room," Susan offered, and she began to put her room in order. The daybed in the playroom was made up for the boys.

Susan and Matt were putting another leaf in the dining room table when they heard their car returning.

They ran to the door and opened it. "Merry Christmas!" they called almost in the same breath.

"Merry Christmas to you," replied their guests.

Then Mr. Harper introduced the family—Mr. and Mrs. Henderson, Jack, Donna, and baby Michael.

"This is very kind of you," said Mrs. Henderson as she shook Mrs. Harper's hand.

"We're all happy to have you," replied Mrs. Harper. "The snowstorm spoiled our plans, too, so we'll have a happy time here together."

It was not long before Mrs. Henderson and Mrs. Harper were busy in the kitchen making last-minute preparations for dinner. Mr. Harper, Mr. Henderson, and the boys went down into the basement.

"I think they're going to make a base for the Christmas tree," Susan confided to Donna as they set the table together.

"Oh! You were able to get a tree in this snowstorm?" Donna's eyes sparkled.

"Yes, dad got it just tonight," Susan replied. "We can trim it after dinner."

Dinner was a happy time. The food was delicious, but best of all, the two families got better acquainted. When it was over, they cleared the table and washed the dishes. Afterwards, they mounted the tree on its base and put it up before the big window in the livingroom.

"It's a beautiful tree!" exclaimed Donna.

Then they all hung lights, tinsel, and ornaments on the branches. The younger boys and girls took care of the lower branches. Baby Michael was there, too, all nestled in his basket-bed watching the workers.

Susan didn't notice when her mother and Mrs. Henderson left the group, but it wasn't long before she smelled delicious odors coming from the kitchen.

"Oh! Cookies!" she cried. "Christmas cookies!"

When the women joined the group again, the tree was all trimmed. The two families stood together and admired it.

"Should I turn out the big lamp now so we can have the Christmas story?" Matt asked.

At a nod from his father, Matt turned out the light. Then he picked up the Bible and handed it to his father. The children all sat on the floor with their parents on chairs behind them.

Mr. Harper began to read, and everyone listened to the old, old story. Susan looked at baby Michael. Having him there seemed to bring that first Christmas right into their own living room.

There was a moment of silence when the story was ended. Then Mrs. Harper began to sing softly "Silent night, holy night," and both families joined in singing. Then, one by one, as was their custom on Christmas Eve, Mr. Harper, Mrs. Harper, Matt, and Susan each said a thank-you prayer for Christmas. Susan prayed, "Thank you, God, for our new friends who are with us. And for grandma and grandpa. Help them to have a happy Christmas, too. Amen."

Animals at the Manger

Rudolf O. Wiemer
Translated by Melva Rorem

I am the Dog. With a shepherd lad
I heard the heavens ring out loud and glad;
Heard angels sing of your birth, dear Lord,
While spellbound we listened to every word.
Then as the shepherds fell down in dread,
"Be not afraid! Come!" the angel said.
The lad and I quickly followed the men
Through the fields, up rough paths, till we found you, and then
We knelt at the manger. You're sleeping there now.
I will keep watch, dear Child. Bow, wow! Bow, wow!

I am the Sheep; I lay fast asleep
While friendly shepherds close watch did keep.
Then all of a sudden a light bright as day
Flashed through the sky, and I heard someone say:
"To the stable, make haste, don't delay!"
One and all we agreed and set out with great speed,
Trusting the stars for the light that we'd need.
Now sheep are not very wise, some suppose,
But the winds can be bitter in wintertime snows,
So we brought our wool for the Christ child's warm clothes!

I am the Ox. Do you know what I'll do?
I'll bring a bundle of straw to you.
You shall not lie in a manger bare;
You shall lie on a pillow, soft as the air.
I'll stand guard at the door; no harm shall you know.
A vigil I'll keep while the winter winds blow.
Outside it is dark, but the great star shines through.
Sleep now, sweet Jesus, while I sing to you:
Moo . . . moo . . . moo. . . .

I am the Mouse. I live in a stall.
I just looked out through a hole in the wall.
I saw village-folk and the Wise Men three
All coming the newborn Child to see.
And there close behind were the animals too;

Why, it almost seems too good to be true!
They are welcomed by Joseph, the doors open wide,
And with his kind greeting they all come inside.
Outside it is gloomy in dark of the night,
But here in the stable there's soft candlelight.
I am the Mouse. I say: Peep, peep!
Little Jesus, I'll keep watch till you're fast asleep!

The Jar of Rosemary

Maud Lindsay

There was once a little prince whose mother, the queen, was sick. All summer she lay in bed, and everything was kept quiet in the palace; but when the autumn came she grew better. Every day brought color to her cheeks and strength to her limbs, and by and by the little prince was allowed to go into her room and stand beside her bed to talk to her.

He was very glad of this, for he wanted to ask her what she would like for a Christmas present; and as soon as he had kissed her and laid his cheek against hers, he whispered his question in her ear.

"What should I like for a Christmas present?" said the queen. "A smile and a kiss and a hug around the neck; these are the dearest gifts I know."

But the prince was not satisfied with this answer. "Smiles and kisses and hugs you can have every day," he said, "but think, mother, think, if you could choose the thing you wanted most in all the world, what would you take?"

"If I might take my choice of all the world I believe a little jar of rosemary like that which bloomed in my mother's window when I was a little girl would please me better than anything else."

The little prince was delighted to hear this, and as soon as he had gone out of the queen's room he sent a servant to his father's greenhouses to inquire for a rosemary plant.

But the servant came back with disappointing news. There were carnation pinks in the king's greenhouses and roses with golden hearts, and lovely lilies; but there was no rosemary. Rosemary was a common herb and grew, mostly, in country gardens, so the king's gardeners said.

"Then go into the country for it," said the little prince. "No matter where it grows, my mother must have it for a Christmas present."

So messengers went into the country here, there, and everywhere to seek the plant, but each one came back with the same story to tell; there was rosemary, enough and to spare, in the spring, but the frost had been in the country and there was not a green sprig left to bring to the little prince for his mother's Christmas present.

Two days before Christmas, however, news was brought that rosemary had been found, a lovely green plant growing in a jar, right in the very city where the prince himself lived.

"But where is it?" said he. "Why have you not brought it with you? Go and get it at once."

"Well, as for that," said the servant who had found the plant, "there is a little difficulty. The old woman to whom the rosemary belongs did not want to sell it even though I offered her a handful of silver for it."

"Then give her a purse of gold," said the little prince.

So a purse filled so full of gold that it could not hold another piece was taken to the old woman, but presently it was brought back. She would not sell her rosemary; no, not even for a purse of gold.

"Perhaps if Your Little Highness would go yourself and ask her, she might change her mind," said the prince's nurse. So the royal carriage drawn by six white horses was brought, and the little prince and his servants rode away to the old woman's house, and when they got there the first thing they spied was the little green plant in a jar standing in the old woman's window.

The old woman herself came to the door, and she was glad to see the little prince. She invited him in, and bade him warm his hands by the fire, and gave him a cookie from her cupboard to eat.

She had a little grandson no older than the prince, but he was sick and could not run about and play like other children. He lay in a little, white bed in the old woman's room, and the little prince, after he had eaten the cookie, spoke to him, and took out his favorite plaything, which he always carried in his pocket, and showed it to him.

The prince's favorite plaything was a ball which was like no other ball that had ever been made. It was woven of magic stuff as bright as the sunlight, as sparkling as the starlight, and as golden as the moon at harvest time. And when the little prince threw it into the air or bounced it on the floor or turned it in his hands it rang like a chime of silver bells.

The sick child laughed to hear it and held out his hands for it, and the prince let him hold it, which pleased the grandmother as much as the child.

But pleased though she was, she would not sell the rosemary. She had brought it from the home where she had lived when her little grandson's father was a boy, she said, and she hoped to keep it till she died. So the prince and his servants had to go home without it.

No sooner had they gone than the sick child began to talk of the wonderful ball.

"If I had such a ball to hold in my hand," he said, "I should be contented all the day."

"You may as well wish for the moon in the sky," said his grandmother; but she thought of what he said, and in the evening when he was asleep she put her shawl around her, and taking the jar of rosemary with her, she hastened to the king's palace.

When she got there the servants asked her errand but she would answer nothing till they had taken her to the little prince.

"Silver and gold would not buy the rosemary," she said when she saw him; "but if you will give me your golden ball for my little grandchild, you may have the plant."

"But my ball is the most wonderful ball that was ever made!" cried the little prince, "and it is my favorite plaything. I would not give it away for anything."

And so the old woman had to go home with her jar of rosemary under her shawl.

The next day was the day before Christmas, and there was a great stir and bustle in the palace. The queen's physician had said that she might sit up to see the Christmas tree that night, and have her presents with the rest of the family; and everyone was running to and fro to get things in readiness for her.

The queen had so many presents, and very fine they were too, that the Christmas tree could not hold them all, so they were put on a table before the throne and wreathed around with holly and with pine. The little prince went in with his nurse to see them, and to put his gift, which was a jewel, among them.

"She wanted a jar of rosemary," he said as he looked at the glittering heap.

"She will never think of it again when she sees these things. You may be sure of that," said the nurse.

But the little prince was not sure. He thought of it himself many times that day, and once, when he was playing with his ball, he said to the nurse, "If I had a rosemary plant I'd be willing to sell it for a purse full of gold. Wouldn't you?"

"Indeed, yes," said the nurse, "and so would anyone else in his right senses. You may be sure of that."

The little boy was not satisfied, though, and presently when he had put his ball up and stood at the window watching the snow which had come to whiten the earth for Christ's birthday, he said to the nurse, "I wish it were spring. It is easy to get rosemary then, is it not?"

"Your Little Highness is like the king's parrot that knows but one word with your rosemary, rosemary, rosemary," said the nurse, who was a little out of patience by that time. "Her Majesty the Queen only asked for it to please you. You may be sure of that."

But the little prince was not sure, and when the nurse had gone to her supper and he was left by chance for a moment alone, he put on his coat of fur, and taking the ball with him, he slipped away from the palace and hastened toward the old woman's house.

He had never been out at night by himself before, and he might have felt a little afraid had it not been for the friendly stars that twinkled in the sky above him.

"We will show you the way," they seemed to say, and he trudged on bravely in their light, till, by and by, he came to the house and knocked at the door.

Now the little sick child had been talking of the wonderful ball all the evening. "Did you see how it shone, grandmother? And did you hear how the little bells rang?" he said, and it was just then that the little prince knocked at the door.

The old woman made haste to answer the knock, and when she saw the prince she was too astonished to speak.

"Here is the ball," he cried, putting it into her hands. "Please give me the rosemary for my mother."

And so it happened that when the queen sat down before her great table of gifts the first thing she spied was a jar of sweet rosemary like that which had bloomed in her mother's window when she was a little girl.

"I should rather have it than all the other gifts in the world," she said, and she took the little prince in her arms and kissed him.

The Mysterious Christmas Gifts

Evelyn S. Wilharm

Ellie shook her piggy bank. "What are you going to get for mom?" asked her younger brother, Michael.

"I don't know yet," Ellie said, shaking some more. She gathered up the nickels, dimes, and quarters as they fell on the bed, and put them into her purse.

It was the day before Christmas Eve. Mother had almost finished her shopping, except for a few last-minute things.

"Everybody ready?" she called, going to get Susan from her crib. "Last call for all Christmas shoppers!"

Mother looked down at Susan's round face pressed against the white sheet. There she lay, all dressed to go out—and fast asleep!

"I hate to wake her," mother said. "I don't think she feels good. She's cutting teeth, and she's cried a lot today. If only someone could stay with her, and just let her sleep—and my shopping would be easier too," she added.

Ellie was listening. She had counted on this shopping trip to get a present for mom and for dad—and for Michael and Susan. In fact, she hadn't done *any* of her Christmas shopping. And she had saved her allowance for weeks. But—

"Mom, I'll stay with Susie," she heard herself saying. She put down her purse and unbuttoned her red coat.

Mother smiled. "Thank you, dear," she said. "It's nice of you to offer, but are you sure you could manage all right?"

"I could if Susie's asleep," Ellie pointed out. "Besides, I'm not a baby. I'm nine!"

"Well, maybe," mother said thoughtfully, going to the telephone.

In a few minutes she came back. "Mrs. Marshall, next door, said she would be home all afternoon doing Christmas baking, so if Susan wakes up and you need help, just call her."

Ellie heard the car back out of the garage, and then mother and Michael zoomed off down the street without her. The house was very still. Susan stirred in her sleep, and Ellie tiptoed into the kitchen to get cookies and milk—and to think.

"*Now* what will I give everyone for Christmas?" she asked herself. She wished she could have gone shopping. She could imagine the crowds of excited people, the brightly lighted Christmas trees, fat red Santas, Christmas music playing, all the beautiful toys. And she *did* want to look again at the record player she was hoping to get.

Oh, well, she told herself, *I must think of something—some gifts for the family.*

But when mother and Michael came home, Ellie still hadn't thought of anything.

They came in loaded with packages which they quickly took to the bedroom to hide. Mother sat down and took off her shoes.

"Whew, am I tired!" she exclaimed. "The stores were so crowded. I was really glad that Susan was at home asleep." She reached down and kissed Ellie on the forehead.

"Did she wake up?"

Ellie shook her head. "She's still sleeping."

Mother smiled. "You've already given *me* a wonderful present today," she said.

"I *did*?" Ellie asked, puzzled.

Mother nodded. "You baby-sat with Susan."

"*That* was a present?"

"Oh, yes," mother assured her. "You know, not all presents come wrapped in paper and tied with ribbon."

Ellie had a sudden idea.

That night when everyone was wrapping gifts and putting them under the tree, Ellie brought out some of the most oddly shaped packages that anyone had ever seen. She placed them carefully under the tree with the others.

"Now what could be in those packages?" mother wondered out loud.

Michael picked his up and shook it. "It doesn't rattle," he said.

Father felt his. "It's bumpy," he observed.

Christmas morning came.

"I'm going to open Ellie's present first," father said. "I want to know what's so bumpy."

"And doesn't rattle," Michael said, picking up his tiny package.

Father untied the ribbon. He slowly unfolded a sheet of notebook paper which had been folded very small, and read, "To dad: Two shoeshines. From Ellie."

Michael opened his package. It was also a sheet of paper, and on it was written, "To Michael: You may play with my skateboard *three* times, and I won't fuss at you. From Ellie."

Mother's gift was folded small, wrapped in red tissue paper, and tied with green ribbon. On hers was written, "To mom: Two more hours of baby-sitting—when you need it. And two errands run—when needed. From Ellie."

Baby Susan's was a whole page filled with XXXXXXXs which, everybody knows, means love and kisses.

Mother looked at father. They both smiled.

"I think Ellie's mysterious gifts are the very best of all," mother said. "Ellie gave us *herself*!"

Who Needs Jim?   Margaret D. Woolington

*I*t was the day before Christmas, and the Johnson house was filled with the odor of cookies baking. The counter in the kitchen was full of big, brown gingerbread men with raisin eyes and green candy noses. Jim's grandmother was busy putting red icing smiles on them when he came in.

"Bet I could do that," he said.

"Oh, I bet you could too," she answered. "But we are in such a hurry, maybe you could help some other time. If you will go play until I finish, then you can lick the bowl."

"But I don't want to play. I want to help," Jim said, and he meant it. Everyone in the house was doing something special for Christmas except him.

"I know you want to help, Jim," his grandmother said as she searched for the cookie cutter. "But there just isn't much a little boy like you can do right now."

There she goes with that little boy stuff again, he thought. *Going to kindergarten hasn't made a bit of difference. I'm still a baby around here.*

He made designs in the white flour on the table. His two sisters were in the dining room making eggshell decorations for the tree. When he had tried to make some, he kept getting glue all over everything, so they chased him out. He couldn't make ornaments for the Christmas tree; he couldn't help make gingerbread cookies. Christmas was for girls, he finally decided. With all the baking and cooking and making things, a boy just got lost in all the confusion.

Even though he enjoyed being in the busy, sweet-smelling kitchen, he could see that he was in the way. So he decided to go watch television if nobody was going to let him help. As he went down the hall, he noticed the basement door was open, and he heard someone sawing down below. *It must be grandfather,* he thought. He was the only other man in the house this afternoon. So Jim went down to see what he was doing.

On the workbench under a bright light was something that looked like a small feeding trough, the kind he had seen on his grandfather's farm. Jim wondered what that had to do with Christmas.

When he finished sawing and stepped back to inspect his work, grandfather almost fell over Jim, who was right behind him.

"Look who's here," he said. "I thought you were upstairs helping with the cookies."

"Aw, that's for girls," Jim said, not mentioning that they all thought he was in the way.

"Well, lucky for me that you came along," his grandfather said, smiling at him. "Will you hold this in place while I nail it?"

"What is it for?" Jim asked.

"I'll show you, but first you have to promise that you can keep a secret. This is going to be a surprise."

Jim told him that he always kept secrets, so grandfather took out some wooden animals from a box beneath the workbench. In the corner of the box, wrapped in a towel, were the three Wise Men, and Mary and Joseph. "I have been carving these all year long," he told Jim.

"But where is the baby Jesus?" Jim asked.

His grandfather searched through the box, and Jim took all the papers out and looked through them. But there was no baby Jesus.

"Well, I will have to make another one. It wouldn't be Christmas without baby Jesus in the manger." Grandfather frowned. "And I still have to finish the manger."

"I could make a baby Jesus," Jim offered. But his grandfather laughed and shook his head.

Jim ran for the stairs, but fell over the unfinished trough on the floor. "Everybody is doing something for Christmas except me!" he shouted. "I can't do anything!"

"Wait, Jim, wait!" Grandfather came over and picked Jim up. "There is something you can do. It will take patience, but it would save me time so I could start making a baby Jesus. Are you interested?"

Grandfather gave Jim a sanding board, and, putting his hand over Jim's, began showing him how to sand the rough corners on the trough.

"I can do it!" Jim said.

"Of course you can," grandfather replied. "You have fine, strong hands. Now I need to find a good piece of wood to make the most important part of our manger scene. He picked up a piece and showed it to Jim. "What do you think about this one?"

Jim inspected it for a minute. "OK," he said, happy that he had at last found a way he could help.

Bobby's Presents

Elsie Duncan Yale

I've just bought a present for mother—
The dandiest baseball, you see;
And if she can't possibly use it,
Why, then, she can lend it to me.

I've bought a fine bat for my father—
I'm sure it will make daddy smile;
And if he thinks he doesn't quite need it,
I'll borrow it once in awhile.

I picked out this jack-knife for baby—
The best on the storekeeper's shelf;
But yet—she might cut herself, maybe!
I think I will keep it myself.

For Aunty I bought some nice candy;
But—I'm really sorry to say,
'Twas up on my bureau so handy,
And now it has vanished away.

Some folks simply hate Christmas shopping;
They're glad when at last it is done.
But I don't see why they feel that way—
I think it's the greatest of fun!

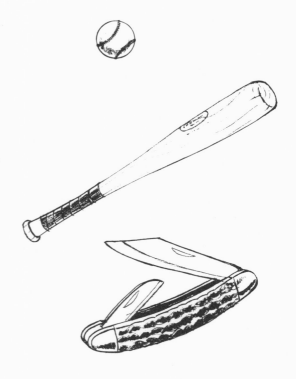

The Legend of the Christmas Rose

Retold by Ron and Lyn Klug

*F*inished with her work, Rachel, the shepherd girl, stepped out of her home at the edge of Bethlehem and hurried down the street. She would have an hour to search before it grew dark. As she peered into windows and through doorways, she prayed a silent prayer, "Lord, help me find the baby!"

Ever since her father had come home with that strange story, she had thought of nothing else. He had told of a choir of angels that sang in the night sky and how he and the other shepherds had hurried to a stable and found the baby, the one called Jesus. How she wished that she could have seen the angels and found the baby!

Rachel was a curious child who always wanted to know about everything. Finally her father gave her permission to go see the baby. But when Rachel came to the stable her father had told her about, the baby and his parents were no longer there. Neither the innkeeper nor his wife had any idea of where they had gone. Rachel had looked and looked, but she could find no trace of them. Somehow she felt that they were still in Bethlehem, so whenever she had a few minutes free from work at home, she wandered the crooked streets. She was determined to find the baby Jesus and kneel before him, as her father had done.

Rachel glanced up. The sky was beginning to grow dark, and the evening star gleamed brightly. Rachel knew she must soon turn toward home. The evening was growing colder, and she wrapped her cloak around herself. Her heart was filled with disappointment. It seemed that she would never find the baby.

Then just ahead of her she heard a commotion. A small procession of travelers moved down the street. The men looked strange and different—*Like kings*, Rachel thought. She crept along the street to get a closer look. In her curiosity, she forgot all about the baby.

She watched until she saw the strangers stop in front of a house and then enter it. She slipped carefully up to the house and peeked in at the window. The three strangers were kneeling in front of a mother and her baby. Rachel's heart told her that this was Jesus, the Christ child. Rachel had found him at last!

She watched as each of the travelers offered the baby a gift. One gave gold. Another gave incense. And the third presented the child with myrrh. These were special gifts indeed!

But I have no gift to give, Rachel thought. *How can I kneel before the baby without a gift? I must find something.* But what could a poor shepherd girl give?

Then she remembered the flowers that grew in the fields around Bethlehem, brightly colored flowers that would make the baby glad.

She ran quickly through the darkening streets to the fields at the edge of the village. She searched and searched, but the winter had been cold, and there were no flowers, not even a green leaf—only scattered patches of snow sparkling in the starlight. Tired and cold and discouraged, Rachel stood alone and wept.

Just then the moon rose in the sky, and its beams glistened on the snow. An angel passing by saw her and was filled with pity. He stooped down and brushed aside the snow at Rachel's feet. Where his wing touched the ground there sprang up clusters of beautiful winter roses, glowing white with pink-tipped petals. Rachel knelt and touched the roses.

"No offering—not even gold or incense or myrrh—is a finer gift for the baby than these pure Christmas roses," said the angel.

Her heart brimming with joy, Rachel gathered the winter roses in her arms and hurried back to the house where she had seen the baby. The three strangers were gone now, but the baby was still there. The mother motioned for Rachel to come in.

Shyly Rachel entered the room. Kneeling before the child, the little shepherd girl offered the bunch of Christmas roses. When the Christ child saw the flowers, he smiled, and Rachel's heart was filled with love.

Tommy's Special Present

Margaret Shauers

Tommy looked across the dinner table at his grandmother. "Just think, Gran," he exclaimed. "Only four more weeks until Christmas. I can hardly wait!"

"You'll have to wait for Christmas," grandmother answered, smiling. "But you won't have to wait for one of your presents. If you'll come to my house after school tomorrow, I'll give you a special Christmas surprise."

"Gran!" Tommy exclaimed eagerly, "What is it?"

"If I told you, it wouldn't be a surprise," she said with a laugh. "Wait until tomorrow."

Tommy thought and thought about the special present. Was it a new basketball? A big dump truck? An electric train?

"I can't wait to see my special present," he told his mother that evening before going to bed. "Did Gran tell you what it is?"

His mother nodded. Then she said, "But I can't tell you either. You'll have to wait and see it for yourself."

But waiting wasn't easy. At school the next day, Tommy thought more about the special present than about math or reading.

At last the bell rang. Tommy grabbed up his books and ran all the way to grandmother's house.

"I'm here," he called as he opened her front door.

"Come into the living room," grandmother called. "Your present is under the Christmas tree."

Tommy hurried down the hall and into the living room. He looked across at the tree.

But there was no gayly wrapped package under the tree—nothing that might hold a train or a truck or a new basketball. The only things under the tree were a small wooden manger, like the one used in church for the Christ child at Christmas, and a little box of hay.

Tommy walked across the room slowly. He couldn't see anything special about an empty manger and a pile of hay. But he didn't want to hurt his grandmother's feelings.

"Is this my present?" he asked as he came up to her.

"Yes, Tommy," she said. "And it's a very special present indeed. Let me tell you a story so you'll understand."

Tommy looked up and saw that grandmother's eyes had that faraway look she got when she was thinking about the "old times" before she'd come to the United States.

"Many years ago," she began, "when I was a girl in Hungary, I had a manger like this and a pile of hay every Advent season. Every time I did a good deed or made someone happy, I put one straw of hay into the manger for the Christ child to sleep on. In Hungary we thought that filling a crib with good deed straws was a good way to show God that we loved others."

Grandmother looked down at Tommy and smiled. "I will have another present for you at Christmastime, but I thought you might like to do the same thing I did when I was your age."

Tommy looked down at the little manger. He thought about the toys he'd hoped to get. But he already had a closet full of toys. And while toys showed that other people loved him, he had nothing to show that he loved others.

He remembered how good he'd felt last summer when he'd helped Mrs. Jones clean her yard. She was old and stiff and couldn't pick things up from the ground. She had been very happy when Tommy helped her. Because she had been happy, Tommy felt happy, too.

Then there was the time when his church school class had given a party at the children's home. Tommy had felt warm and nice inside, knowing he'd helped bring the children joy.

He thought for a moment longer about the things he could do during Advent. He could run errands for Mrs. Jones and for other neighbors. He could fill up a box of clothing and toys for the children at the children's home. He could help his parents and be nicer to his little sister. He could—

why, there was no end to the things he could do.

Tommy looked up at grandmother and his eyes were shining. "It's a wonderful present," he said. "I'll work hard to fill the manger with hay before Christmas Day."

Then he smiled. "It won't be very hard work. Making people happy makes me happy, too."

Words from an Old Spanish Carol

Ruth Sawyer

*Shall I tell you who will come
to Bethlehem on Christmas morn,
who will kneel them gently down
before the Lord, newborn?*

*One small fish from the river,
with scales of red, red gold,
one wild bee from the heather,
one grey lamb from the fold,
one ox from the high pasture,
one black bull from the herd,
one goatling from the far hills,
one white, white bird.*

*And many children—God give them grace,
bringing tall candles to light Mary's face.*

*Shall I tell you who will come
to Bethlehem on Christmas morn,
who will kneel them gently down
before the Lord, newborn?*

Christmas on the Prairie Kit Lambeth

Mother, we have company!" Mary Beecher shouted. She pulled back the oilcloth curtain and watched her father greet them.

"They must be nearly frozen, riding in that open wagon," Mrs. Beecher replied. "Mary, you and Amy watch the pudding. I'll get extra blankets."

"There's scarcely enough pudding for the four of us, much less for company," Amy Beecher grumbled. She jabbed the hasty pudding angrily and sent a generous portion over the side of the kettle into the open fire.

"Now look what you did," Mary scolded.

"I don't care!" Amy said stoutly. "I'm tired of living in a sod house, having so little to eat and nothing to read."

"It's Christmas Eve, Amy. Let's think about all the good things we do have," said Mrs. Beecher.

Before Amy could answer, the three tired strangers plodded in. They were so cold they had to be helped over to the fire.

"Pour some hot tea, Amy," Mr. Beecher ordered. "That will warm them a little."

"Father, we have only a little tea left in the—" Amy's words trailed off when father shook his head.

The strangers had traveled all day, hoping to reach their homestead in central Kansas by Christmas morning. "Hansen's our name," the man said between great gulps of tea. "Elga here is about your daughter's age," he added, patting the blanketed form beside him. "She sure wanted to be home for Christmas."

"You can't travel in weather like this," said Mr. Beecher. "You're welcome to spend the night here."

"Our provisions are low, but you're welcome to share what little we have," Mrs. Beecher offered.

Everyone finally agreed and the Hansen family prepared to spend the night. As soon as breakfast was over the next morning, they would be on their way.

Mary was so excited about the unexpected company she'd forgotten the gift she was finishing. She invited Elga and Amy to help her.

Elga unwrapped herself from the blanket and slowly followed Mary and Amy to a little room curtained off from the rest of the house.

"This will be your first Christmas on the prairie!" Mary exclaimed. "How exciting."

"It's our second one. And we have even less than we did last year," Amy said sourly. "Some Christmas this will be."

"L-e-t-'s b-e n-i-c-e." Mary spelled the words in a whisper, hoping Elga wouldn't hear.

"Don't you spell at me, Mary Beecher," Amy hissed. "And stop pretending to be so happy. I know you want a Christmas tree just as much as I do."

Amy was right. Mary wanted a Christmas tree more than anything else this year. It just wouldn't seem like Christmas without one. But there wasn't a tree of any kind here on the prairie, just tumbleweeds and gophers. Mary had decided long ago, however, that she must not spoil her family's happiness by demanding things she couldn't have. "Mother says God gives us everything we need. Maybe, if we really look for a tree and truly believe we will find one, God will help us," she said cheerfully. She took her yarn and began knitting.

"Making mittens for father helps you to forget our problems, but what about me?" asked Amy. "I've nothing to give anyone."

"You have to be resourceful to live on the prairie, Amy."

"I don't even know what re—re—that word means," said Amy.

"It means to solve your problems with what you have."

Just then Mr. Beecher pulled back the dividing curtain and smiled at Mary, who quickly hid her yarn and mittens behind her.

"We need chips for the fire," said Mr. Beecher. "Gather them before dark. Elga, come stay by the fire while the girls do their chores."

"I hope you find your Christmas tree," Elga whispered.

Mary was already dressed to go outdoors. "Better take off your hair ribbon. You'll lose it in the wind," she warned Amy.

"My cap will cover it," Amy said confidently. Besides, it's the only nice thing I have. I want to wear it on Christmas Eve."

Opening the door, Mary stepped out into the cold prairie wind. Suddenly, she gasped with delight. "Look, it's snowing!"

Both girls stood for a moment, watching the bare brown earth change into a white wonderland. Even the tumbleweeds sparkled against the light of the lantern. Mary pointed to a tumbleweed caught in a wagon wheel. "That will be our Christmas tree," she shouted.

Carefully, Mary and Amy pulled the tumbleweed from between the spokes of the wheel. Their next problem was finding a place to put their tree until the next morning.

"The snow will melt if we take it inside," Amy said. "Why don't we keep it in the stable. We'll use one of father's feed buckets to stand it in."

"That's a good idea," answered Mary. "We can trim it after supper."

"Let's make a rule that each ornament must tell a part of the Christmas story. We'll share it with the Hansens," Amy suggested. "Our 'story tree' will be our gift to Elga and her family."

"Now you're being resourceful," Mary replied.

"I am?" asked Amy. "You never said it could be fun."

As soon as the girls gathered chips for the fire, they began collecting ornaments for their tree. Mary found bits of gold-colored yarn in her knitting basket. She also made a garland out of the precious bittersweet berries she'd saved to make a necklace.

Amy wandered about the room, unable to find anything to put on the tree. She untied her cap and flung it on the bed in disgust. Just then her yellow ribbon fell to the floor. Quickly, she picked it up and placed it with Mary's collection. "We can make a star for our tree with this," she said softly.

"But that's your only ribbon. Are you sure you want to use it?"

"You gave up your berries, so I'll give up my ribbon. It's the only thing I have for our tree."

After supper was over, Mary and Amy excused themselves and raced out to the stable, their pockets bulging with ornaments. Amy packed snow in the bucket as Mary held the tree straight. Then they began to decorate it. Amy's yellow ribbon had been tied to wire twisted in the shape of a star. It went on first.

"A star guided the shepherds to where baby Jesus was born," Mary said solemnly. Then she laid her garland of red berries around the tumbleweed.

"And later the Wise Men brought precious gifts to Jesus," Amy stated. "And these berries were precious to you."

"All we have left are the bows I made from my yarn," said Mary.

"They're gold-colored, and the Wise Men brought a gift of gold to the young child Jesus."

At last the tree was trimmed. The girls stepped back to admire it.

It was dark when Mary and Amy walked back to the house.

"Where have you been?" Elga asked, when all three girls were tucked in bed.

Mary and Amy couldn't keep from giggling. They were so excited they just knew they couldn't wait till morning to surprise Elga. But all they said was, "We had chores to finish."

On Christmas morning, before anyone awakened, Mary and Amy slipped out to the stable and brought their tree into the house. Very quietly, they sat it in the corner away from the fireplace. Mary placed beneath the tree her father's mittens and a scarf she'd knitted for her mother. Both girls then scrambled back into bed.

Before long they heard their father call out a hearty "Merry Christmas, everyone!"

Fully dressed and wide awake, Mary and Amy tumbled out of bed and followed Elga.

"Oh, how beautiful," Elga whispered. She stood perfectly still, ignoring the gifts Mr. and Mrs. Hansen had for her; she saw nothing but the sparkling tumbleweed, red garland, and the yellow star.

"Tell us the Christmas story, father," Mary begged.

Mr. Beecher told the story as he pointed to each ornament. "This tree could tell the Christmas story all by itself," he said, laughing.

Amy went over and stood by Elga. "We had to keep the tree in the stable last night so it would be a surprise," she said. "We want you to take it to your new home."

Mary realized how hard it was for Amy to give up her only ribbon, which stood proudly at the top of the tree in the form of a star. How happy she was that Amy had learned the true meaning of Christmas. Amy had given a gift out of love just as the baby Jesus was given to us out of God's love.

Andy's Christmas Prayer

Margaret Shauers

Andy was worried. It was almost Christmas and he had no money to buy his parents a present.

"Dear God," he prayed. "Please help me find a way to get money. I can't find anyone who will pay me to do anything. You're the only one who can help me. Amen."

When he had crawled into bed, he thought about his prayer. Andy had learned at church that God always answers prayers in one way or another. He hoped God would answer this one soon.

Two days went by. Every night Andy asked God to help him get money. By the third day, he was becoming worried again.

Christmas is almost here, he thought as he walked home from school. *God better do something quick.* Just then, Andy looked down. There, lying partially covered with snow, was a 10-dollar bill!

Andy picked it up and wiped it off. Even as he touched it, he could hardly believe it was real. When he'd prayed for money, he'd never thought God would send 10 whole dollars!

Wow! he thought. *I can buy a really nice present with this.* "Thank you very much, God," he said before running the rest of the way home. Perhaps mom would take him shopping right away.

But by the time he reached his house, Andy couldn't make himself go inside. Instead, he stood on the porch feeling confused.

"This money doesn't belong to me," he thought. "Not really."

He tried to tell himself not to be silly, that God had sent the money in answer to his prayer. But he knew someone had lost it, so it couldn't really be his.

I don't know who lost it, he thought. *But I know where I found it.* It had been lying right in front of old Mr. Johnson's house. And Andy's dad had told him once that Mr. Johnson had very little money. What if the 10 dollars belonged to Mr. Johnson? He might need it for food.

Slowly Andy walked back down the block. He knew what he had to do.

"Mr. Johnson," he said when the old man answered the door. "Did you lose 10 dollars?"

Mr. Johnson looked down at Andy as if he couldn't believe what he heard.

Andy held out the bill. "I found it in the snow, right in front of your house."

"Thank God!" Mr. Johnson said as he reached for the bill. "I prayed that I would find it, and God sent you to help me. Come in! Come in!"

Andy walked in the room and looked around. The furniture was old, and a plateful of beans—Mr. Johnson's supper—lay steaming on the table.

Andy swallowed hard. "I have to go, Mr. Johnson," he said. "I'm glad I found the money for you."

"Wait," said Mr. Johnson. "I can't afford to give you money as a reward. But maybe you would like this."

The old man reached behind a chair and pulled out a big object made of wood. "It's not much," he said, handing it to Andy. "It's just one of the figures I whittle from wood to keep me busy."

Andy looked at the wooden figure. It was a carving of a dog, so perfect it almost looked real. "It's beautiful, Mr. Johnson!" he said. "It will make a great Christmas present for my parents!"

As Andy walked home, he kept stopping to look at the wooden dog. *I'll bet you couldn't buy one as nice as this for 10 dollars*, he thought. Then his eyes widened as he had another thought. When his mother's friends saw this dog, they might want to buy some like it. Mr. Johnson could make some money!

"Thanks, God," he prayed. "You sent me a present for mom and dad and help for Mr. Johnson. I'm glad you answered my prayer the way you did!"

Happy Oxen

Annette Wynne

Happy oxen in a stall,
Being there the first of all.

Happy Mother, Mary mild,
Holding close the wondrous Child.

Happy Shepherds on a hill,
Watching as the night grew still.

Happy Wise Men journeying far,
Underneath the strange new star.

Happy lowly cattle shed,
Where the Lord Christ laid his head.

Happy bells that ring again—
Glory to God and peace to men.

Happy Children, all who sing,
Welcome little Baby King!

Annelise and the Wooden Shoe

A German Folktale   **Retold by Ron and Lyn Klug**

Once upon a time, long ago in Germany, a girl named Annelise lived with her grandmother in a tiny hut at the edge of a great forest. They lived by picking up fallen branches and selling them to the people in the village nearby. They had a small garden where they grew a few potatoes and turnips and onions. Although they had little money, they were very happy together.

Grandmother was old, and bent over as she walked. Throughout the countryside and in the village, grandmother was well loved, because she often tended those who were sick and brought a little food to those in need. Perhaps it was from her that Annelise had learned to be so kind. The little girl was as cheerful as a sunbeam and as happy as the chickadees that sang in the pine trees.

One day just a week before Christmas Annelise went with her grandmother to the village to sell their bundle of sticks. There Annelise looked in the store windows and saw the knit dolls, the woolly lambs, and the painted wooden soldiers. Because they were so poor, Annelise had never owned a toy in her life.

That night after their supper of boiled potatoes, Annelise cleared the dishes and swept the floor. Then she sat down at her grandmother's side and asked, "What do you think I will get for Christmas, grandma?"

"Oh, child, child," the old woman said. "There will be no Christmas presents for you. We are too poor."

"But think of all the beautiful toys we saw in the village," the little girl replied. "There are surely enough for every child."

"Those are for people who have money to spend for them," grandmother explained.

"Well, then, maybe some of the children who live in the big house at the end of the village will share some of their toys with me," Annelise said hopefully.

"Dear child," said grandmother, leaning forward and stroking the girl's soft hair. "Your heart is full of love, but other children think only of what they are going to get at Christmas, and they forget about anyone else." She sighed and shook her head. "You may do what you can to make Christmas happy, but do not expect any presents for yourself."

"I know what I'll do," said Annelise. "I will take some fresh pine branches to the sick man who lives by the mill. And then I will pray to the Christ child. Surely he will bring me a gift!"

"Poor child! Poor child!" was all that grandmother could say.

The days passed quickly, and soon it was the morning of Christmas Eve. While grandmother went to the village with a load of sticks, Annelise skipped off to the forest to prepare a surprise for her.

When the old woman came trudging home that night, she found the frame of the doorway covered with green pine branches. And there by the door stood Annelise. "It's to welcome you," the girl said. "The branches are saying 'Merry Christmas.' "

Grandmother smiled and hugged Annelise. Together they opened the door and went in. Here was another surprise. Annelise had trimmed the four posts of the wooden bed with small pine branches. At each side of the fireplace she had placed a bouquet of red mountain-ash berries.

Forgetting how tired she was, grandmother laughed and clapped her hands.

After supper Annelise sat by grandmother's side, and the old woman told again the story of the birth of the Christ child. Although Annelise had heard the story many times before, she never grew tired of it.

When grandmother finished, she said, "Now, Annelise, it is time to go to bed." Grandmother pulled off her heavy wooden shoes and placed them before the fireplace.

"Grandmother, don't you think some kind person in the village will remember us and bring us a Christmas present?" Annelise asked.

"No," said grandmother sadly. "I'm afraid no one will."

"Well, then, the Christ child will," Annelise replied. "I'm going to put one of your wooden shoes on the window sill so he can leave a gift."

"Oh, poor child," murmured grandmother. "You will only be disappointed. Tomorrow morning there will be nothing at all in the shoe."

But hope still glowed in the heart of Annelise. She opened the door of the little hut and stepped out into the darkness. A cold wind was blowing, and she could feel soft flakes of snow in the air. Standing on tiptoe, Annelise placed her grandmother's wooden shoe on the window sill. She was soon back inside, warming herself by the fire.

That night when the two went quietly to bed, Annelise prayed to the heavenly Father, thanking him for sending the Christ child into the world. Soon she was fast asleep.

The next morning very early, before the sun was up, Annelise was awakened by the sound of singing from the village. She knew it was the choir boys caroling in the streets, as they did each year on Christmas Day.

Springing out of bed, she dressed as quickly as she could. Then she unfastened the door and hurried out to see what the Christ child had left in the wooden shoe.

It had snowed all night, and now a white blanket covered everything. The world looked like a fairyland. Annelise climbed onto a large stone beneath the window and carefully lifted down the wooden shoe. Brushing off the snow, she peeked inside. Then with her heart pounding, she ran back to grandmother.

"Oh, see what the Christ child left!" Annelise exclaimed. "Isn't it beautiful?"

Grandmother stepped forward to see what the little girl was holding in her hands. It was a tiny chickadee, whose wing had evidently been broken in the night's storm. It had found shelter in the toe of the wooden shoe.

Grandmother gently took the chickadee from Annelise's hands and carefully bound the broken wing. She showed Annelise how to make a warm nest for the little bird close beside the fire. When breakfast was ready, she let Annelise feed the bird a few moist crumbs.

Later that day Annelise carried some fresh green pine branches to the sick, old man who lived by the mill. When she returned home, she found the little bird asleep. Soon, however, he opened his eyes and stretched his neck as if to say, "It's time for me to eat again."

Annelise gladly fed him, and then, holding him in her lap, gently stroked his feathers. The little bird winked his eyes and turned his head from side to side in such a funny way that Annelise laughed until tears came.

Lovingly she placed the bird back in the little nest by the fireplace. She went to grandmother and, putting her arms around the old woman, whispered, "What a beautiful Christmas, grandmother! Is there anything in the world better than Christmas?"

"No, my child," said grandmother, "not to such a loving heart as yours."

Merry Christmas, Maria

Mona K. Guldswog

Maria huddled closer into her sweater as the wind flung a curtain of snow against the window pane. It was hard to pay attention to the day's lesson when she felt so cold inside and out. Her thoughts traveled across the many, many miles separating her from her family.

Did they miss her way down there in sunny Mexico? Did they say, "Christmas is a lonely time without our Maria?" Or did they picture her surrounded by laughing friends? And did they dance throughout the kitchen, eyes bright with happiness that their Maria had been offered the chance to stay up north and continue her education when the family moved on to follow the harvest?

The sun had been a golden ball in the summer sky when they had said good-bye. She had watched them pile into the truck—mama, papa, Carmen, Ramon, Pedro, José, and little Angel. Maria had stood by Aunt Rosa (not really her aunt, but a good friend of mama's who stayed all year as a housekeeper at the Merrill ranch), waving them happily on their way, her mind filled with visions of all those lovely books to be read waiting for her on the cool of Aunt Rosa's sun porch, away from the heat of the fields. This was to be her chance, and

oh, how proud she would make them all!

But she hadn't known on that summer day just how long a year would be, how very long before that fruit would once again ripen and the trucks roll back with the rollicking sounds of guitar and singing, laughter, fingers flying throughout the day, and feet set to dancing throughout the starry nights.

Maria looked around the classroom. The boys and girls had been kind to her. They had helped her with her halting English and invited her into their homes. But now, nearing Christmas, they were all so very busy with their own private plans, their special ways of celebrating this holiest of days, and she was once again the outsider.

She would have loved helping them all prepare for the class party, but she thought, *They probably feel I wouldn't know how.* Still, the cold settled in her heart as she walked down the hall and heard the happy cluster of boys and girls fall silent when she neared them. It was good so much of her time was spent in study. It helped keep her busy, and it crowded out some of the loneliness.

The bell rang, scattering her thoughts, and she guiltily gathered up her books. She wouldn't make her parents proud of her if she spent all her time daydreaming!

"See you tomorrow, Maria!" said Suzy with the red hair and freckles.

"Don't forget the party!" David called as he stepped quickly through the door.

Maria nodded, trying to keep her smile from slipping. They couldn't know how much she was missing her own kind of Christmas party. She almost wished something would happen to prevent her from coming in to school from the ranch tomorrow, but a blizzard would ruin everyone's plans, and she didn't want that.

The next day dawned clear and sparkling. The sun made the fields look as though they were dusted in diamonds. The wind whipped flying scarfs of snow across the road in front of them as Maria and her "aunt" drove into town. Aunt Rosa sang snatches of old, familiar Christmas songs all the way, and the cold did not seem quite as bitter as before.

"Thank you, Aunt Rosa," Maria said as they reached the school. Maria could tell by the woman's eyes that she knew Maria was thanking her for the loving care and the warm understanding more than for just the morning ride.

Aunt Rosa smiled and reached over to pinch the girl's cheek affectionately. "Don't thank me, little one. There are many who love you. And you are about to discover just how many!" she added mysteriously.

Maria walked quietly up the broad steps to the school, wondering what Aunt Rosa had meant. *I am growing to be just like this northern country,* Maria thought as she glanced around her. *Cold as the wind and lonely as each snowflake flung far from its brothers and sisters to settle in a snowbank.*

The morning passed slowly, even with shortened lessons. Then it was afternoon and time for the party.

Everyone was laughing and joking as they lined up to make their way to the community room. *It's as though they all share some special secret,* thought Maria.

The wide doors were opened, and the group in front of her parted, propelling Maria to the very front of the line. Then, on a happy, laughing wave of children, she was inside.

She couldn't believe her eyes! It was all there—the bright colors, the candles, the little sugar cakes, the spicy cookies, and, yes, it was there too— the fat and cheerful piñata hanging from the ceiling, gently whirling, just ready for the bursting!

Maria looked around her at the boys and girls, from one shining face to another. They had planned all this—for *her!*

"Merry Christmas, Maria! Merry

Christmas!" The cheerful greeting rose from the many smiling faces.

And there, in a crowded room far away from sunny Mexico, but surrounded by love, Christmas came.

Her eyes sparkling with happy tears, Maria swallowed past the tight place in her throat, opened wide her arms to include them all, and said what sprang from her overflowing heart. "Merry Christmas, my new friends. God bless you all!"

Celebrating Christmas around the World

Ron and Lyn Klug

In December children all around the world get ready for Christmas. They do many of the same things you do: visit relatives and friends, go to church, sing songs, exchange presents, make Christmas cookies and candy, and eat a special meal on Christmas Day.

Children in Latin America, south of the United States, don't have frost, snow, or sleigh bells for Christmas. Where they are, December is summertime. If you lived there, on Christmas Eve in the daytime your relatives would gather to eat roast pig, hot chocolate, and cakes. In the afternoon you might go on a picnic, to a bullfight, or swimming at the beach. You might also put on a special costume and walk in a children's parade, singing Christmas songs.

The day for giving and receiving presents is not December 25, as it is here, but January 6, 12 days later. And instead of hanging up your stocking, you would put your shoes out to be filled with toys and candy.

In Brazil you would set up your manger scene early in December. Every day the three Wise Men would be moved closer to the manger. On Christmas Eve the baby Jesus, who has been hidden away, is placed in the manger. People exchange gifts and sing songs.

Mexicans have something we don't have at Christmas—flowers—and on December 16 they decorate their homes with flowers, greens, and colored paper lanterns.

On Christmas Eve they have a party. A piñata filled with candy, fruit, nuts, and little gifts is hung by a rope from the ceiling. All the children are blindfolded and take turns hitting the piñata with a stick. When the prizes fall on the floor, everyone scrambles to get some.

If you were a child in Austria, you wouldn't even see your Christmas tree until Christmas Eve. Your parents would keep it in a locked room and sneak in to decorate it. After dinner on Christmas Eve and the reading of the Christmas story, the door would be opened, and you would see the tree covered with decorations and lights, with all the presents underneath.

Do you have a manger scene made from wood or paper? In an Italian village about 800 years ago, Saint Francis used real animals and real people to create a live manger scene so that people could see what the birth of Jesus was really like. The idea spread to many other countries, and artists began to create scenes with miniature figures that people could have in their homes.

In Africa many boys and girls study at schools run by missionaries. They can't go home for Christmas, because it's too far. If you lived at a mission school in Liberia, weeks before Christmas you would begin saving money for the Christmas offering and your own shopping. Beads and sugar are the things you might buy first—then peanuts, cooked beans, oil, rice, and salt.

For a Christmas tree your school would have a palm tree with the long trunk cut off, decorated with red bells.

Early in the morning on Christmas Day the children sing "Silent Night," say their prayers, and eat breakfast. Then they receive gifts. A girl your age might get a new dish, a piece of cloth for a dress, some soap, or a bit of candy. There would also be a program, something like the ones you have in Sunday school, in which the children act out the Christmas story and sing songs.

Christmas dinner is held outside. You would sit in a circle on the grass and eat rice, beef, and cookies from your new dish. After the meal you might play games, and after dark enjoy the most exciting thing of all—fireworks.

All around the world children celebrate Christmas in many different ways—but they all remember the birth of Jesus in Bethlehem almost 2000 years ago.

Sing for Joy!

A Psalm

Sing for joy to the Lord, all the earth;
*   praise him with songs and shouts of joy!*
Sing praises to the Lord!
*   Play music on the harps!*
Blow the trumpets and horns,
*   and shout for joy to the Lord, our king.*

—Psalm 98:4-6

Kurt Finds Christmas

Nelda Johnson Liebig

Kurt stood at the windows of the empty schoolroom and watched the swirling snow.

Grandfather put his hand on Kurt's shoulder and said, "I can't fly in this weather, but these Alaskan blizzards can be over in a few hours."

"Or they can last days," added Kurt sadly. He wouldn't have come if he had known they couldn't get home for Christmas Eve.

Mrs. Allen, the teacher, came in with an Eskimo boy about Kurt's age. "This is Tingook, one of my fourth graders. He wants you to go to his house, Kurt."

Tingook smiled so wide his eyes were narrow lines in his round face. "Hi! I'm glad you are on our island. We don't have many visitors."

Kurt trudged through the snow behind Tingook. There was grandfather's small plane tied securely against the wind. He wished he could get in it and fly home.

He groped along the foot of the hill. Small houses stuck out like bumps in the snow on the hillside above him. Tingook entered a man-made tunnel in the side of the hill. At the end of the tunnel he scrambled up the rocky wall and pulled himself through a hole in a wooden platform. Puzzled, Kurt followed. He was in a small house. The hole—or entrance to Tingook's home—was in the center of the floor.

Tingook's grandmother smiled at Kurt as she sat in a corner sewing skins.

He was so curious that he forgot all about homesickness—at least for awhile.

Tingook's mother gave the boys strips of dried salmon. Kurt nibbled at his, not sure he would like it. Surprised that it tasted so good, he ate several pieces and thanked Tingook's mother again. As he took off his parka, his harmonica fell out of a pocket. Tingook picked it up and stared at it.

"What is its name?" asked Tingook's mother shyly.

"Name? Oh, it's a harmonica," said Kurt. He played a few notes of "Jingle Bells." Tingook's mother, father, and grandmother listened with happy smiles.

"Play more!" begged Tingook.

Kurt played "Silent Night" and "O Come All Ye Faithful."

Tingook's father pulled on his parka.

"It is time to go to church now," he said.

"The Christmas Eve program!" Tingook explained to Kurt.

As they entered the little wooden church, Kurt said, "It looks like every Eskimo in Alaska is here."

Tingook laughed. "No one in the village would miss the Christmas program."

Kurt thought about his family. They would be in church now. His heart ached. He wanted to be there with them. He squeezed by several adults and sat on the floor near the front.

"I have to put on my shepherd's costume now," whispered Tingook.

Kurt felt all alone—even in the crowded church. He tried to listen to

the songs and recitations, but he thought of home. Next, the nativity scene was set up. It looked just like the one in his church. He swallowed a lump in his throat.

Tingook's father stood up and said, "We are happy to have guests from Anchorage here to share Christmas with us. We hope Kurt will play 'Silent Night' to close our program."

Kurt clutched his harmonica in his pocket and wished he could run. Then he saw grandfather smile and nod encouragement from across the room. Everyone was waiting. Slowly he walked to the front.

The lights were switched off and only a hidden flashlight in the manger gave light. Kurt was glad it was dark because he didn't want to see people watching him. He stared at the manger as he played, thankful he had started without a mistake. He knew Joseph and Mary looked as they would in Christmas programs everywhere. A warm feeling filled his heart. The people and the village didn't seem strange anymore. He played better than he had ever played before.

"I'm proud of you, Kurt," said grandfather as they walked to the school where they would sleep. "For a homesick boy, you played very well."

Kurt thought a minute. "You know something? I don't have to be home to feel Christmas."

"Good! Now you know that Christmas is in the heart—not in a certain city or village."

Grandfather studied the Arctic sky. "It is clearing. I think we will be flying home for your mother's Christmas dinner tomorrow."

The Patchwork Skirt   Alice Sullivan Finlay

Sally blinked back a tear as she looked out the window. The wind rattled the pane. There would be no snow for Christmas again this year. A gust of cold wind blew, and a whisp of air slipped through the window pane. She shivered. She would have started to cry, except for her grandmother. The holiday was bad enough without her grandmother feeling bad, too. But a sudden sniffle gave her away.

"Are you still upset?" asked her grandmother. The lump in Sally's throat didn't allow her to answer. She shook her head without turning around. "Christmas is what you make of it," said her grandmother. "It's in your heart."

"Yes, grandma," she said. In her head, she knew that was true enough, but in her heart, she didn't have the Christmas spirit. How could she when her mother was sick and in the hospital? Every Christmas since she could remember, the whole family did everything together. They bought the tree, decorated it, wrapped gifts, went to church. This year would be different. Mother would be missing.

Maybe I could get a tree by myself, thought Sally. That wouldn't be much fun. Her brother, Tad, stayed upstairs most of the time listening to music. What did he care?

She turned around and watched grandma working on the patchwork quilt. She had worked on it for months now, and it would be the family's Christmas present from her. Sally's dad walked into the living room looking rather distracted.

"Where's my briefcase, Sally?" he asked.

"I'll get it," she answered. She ran to the den and retrieved it. She was trying to be helpful, but she knew she couldn't take her mother's place. Her father brushed her cheek with a kiss, and it was a near miss. Then he rushed out of the house.

The way he acts, you would never know Christmas was almost here, thought Sally. *Some Christmas!*

She went upstairs to see if Tad wanted any dinner. He didn't even hear her open the door. She raised her voice so he could hear her over his headset. "Tad!" she called. Then she shouted louder, "Tad!"

Her brother looked surprised and took off the earphones. "What do you want?"

"Grandma's going to get dinner."

"OK, call me when it's ready." He flipped over on the bed. Sally stood still. "This is going to be some Christmas," she said. "You want to go get a tree?"

Tad looked at her as if she were crazy. He rolled his eyes. "You kidding? With mom in the hospital, there's no point. Besides, when you get older, Christmas is just Christmas. It isn't the same."

Sally fought back the tears and ran to her room. His words stung. She hoped she never got too old for Christmas. She threw herself on the bed and cried until there were no tears left.

"Dear God," she prayed, "all I want this Christmas is for our family to be together again. Help me to help in whatever way I can." A sense of peace came over her as if she could actually feel God near. Then she went downstairs to help with dinner.

Tad was making a pest of himself in the kitchen. "Hey, I'm sorry I yelled at you. Grandma says you're pretty sad about Christmas this year. I guess I'm feeling sort of the same way."

"It's OK," said Sally.

Tad's face brightened. "It won't be OK until we go get that tree. Do you know where the ornaments are?"

Sally beamed, her first smile all day. "In the attic. Can we get the tree tonight?" Tad nodded.

When the tree was decorated, the bulbs cast a warm glow in the room. The whole house felt much more like Christmas. Sally's dad came in the front door.

"Well, I'm glad to see you two haven't forgotten Christmas. Mother will be coming home the day before—the doctor just told me."

Sally cheered. "Mom won't have to do a thing until she's better. That's one of my Christmas presents to her."

"Same here," said Tad.

Grandma chimed in, "We'll all help. Now, too bad you couldn't make something special for your mom."

"Like what?" asked Sally. Then she added, "There's hardly any time."

Grandma had a twinkle in her eye. "We'll have time if we make it a family project," she said. "How about a patchwork skirt, with material from all of you?"

"Sounds great," said Sally, and she immediately began to collect the fabric. First she found an old skirt of her mother's. Then her father gave her a few old ties. From Tad, she got a bright golden shirt. She found her own green silky blouse. It had been her favorite, and she knew her mother would love to see it in the skirt. Grandma chose some of her quilting fabric. They all worked together in the evenings, and by the time mother was to arrive home, the skirt was finished.

Mother's face glowed when she saw the tree. As soon as she was settled in a chair, the family gave her the patchwork skirt.

"It's for you to wear when you get well," Sally explained. "There's something in it from everyone. And we all made it."

There were tears in her mother's eyes. "It's beautiful," she said. She gave Sally a tight hug. "I've missed you. And you, Tad."

Christmas was wonderful. *Thank you, God*, Sally thought. *I got the one special gift that I wanted.*

Until the Grass Sprouts

Ron Matthies

George Henry scraped his fingers down the windowpane, until the frost flaked off and melted on the ledge. Outside—he could see through the two holes his fingers made—outside it was white. The snow stretched as far as he could see. Back beyond the hill. Hanging on the trees. It gave no promise of melting.

He sighed and turned from the window. After flipping the TV knobs six times and finding only soap operas, he stretched on the floor and tried to color. But every picture on every page was colored. He'd even put black lines, dark and heavy, around each picture. Then, he took his cerulean blue and snapped it—first the point, then the middle, right between the R and the U.

From the kitchen, his mother called, "George Henry, what are you doing?"

"Breaking crayons," he said.

"Oh," she said. "That's good."

But in a few minutes her heels scrunched down the hall and she said, "Why? That's a silly thing to do."

"I'm sick of everything. There's nothing to do," he answered.

"Go outside." She tucked her hair back into its ribbon. "Build a snowman."

"Ish," he said. "I've built 500 snowmen this winter."

"Go sliding." She turned the TV off. It was just humming grey dots.

"My sled's broken."

"Build a fort." She pinched crayon crumbs from the carpet.

"We already have more forts than the army," he said.

"Well, stay in then," she said and went back to the kitchen.

It wasn't that George Henry hated winter. It wasn't that at all. But when the snow piled and blew through December, and repiled and blew through January and February, then turned grey and dust-colored in March, it was then he sighed and scraped the frost and wished for melting and buds on the bare branches and mud to ooze between the toes.

It was then that he punched Tubby in the stomach and shouted, "No. I don't want to play fox and geese." It was then he hid behind the bare-branch bushes and pelted Lucy Dermatt with snowballs on her way back from piano lessons. It was then, in the night that flopped down across the afternoon, that he laid on his bed and counted the ceiling squares—99, 100, 101. They always came out to 103.

The doorbell rang. He heard the

door click and the wind blow and his mother mumbling downstairs. She said, "George Henry, Tubby's here."

He didn't answer.

"Come down here," she said.

He didn't answer.

Feet pounded up the steps. It was Tubby. He unwrapped his scarf and covered his cheeks to warm them. "What are you doing?"

"Counting," George Henry said.

"You want to go outside?" Tubby picked mitten lint from his fingernails.

"No," he answered.

"What do you want?" Tubby said.

"To run away." He rolled off the bed. "You want to run away with me?"

"Where?" Tubby asked.

"Florida or the equator. Anyplace it's warm."

"I like it here," Tubby said.

"You're dumb," George Henry answered.

Tubby left. When he was gone, George Henry grabbed his toy bag from the closet, stuffed old clothes down its mouth, and pounded down the stairs. He pulled on his overshoes and shouted, "I'm leaving."

The wind scraped his face, bit between his sleeve and his mitten. The snow packed hard against his feet and wouldn't move. He was puffing by the corner. Six blocks from home he started to cry. But the tears froze on his cheeks. He turned around.

Back home, he didn't take off his overshoes, but let them puddle in the hall. "I'm back," he said.

"Where have you been?" his mother asked.

"I ran away," he said. "But it was too cold."

His mother said, "Take off your overshoes." She examined the wet spots they were making on the carpet.

"I wanted to be warm," he said.

"Spring will come," she smiled.

"Hah. It will not," he snorted. "I decided one thing outside."

"What's that?" she asked and watched an overshoe stream run down the carpet.

"I'm not going to Sunday school anymore."

"Why not?" she asked.

"Not until God makes spring come. I figure if he can hold out, so can I."

"You don't make bargains with God," she said.

"I already have," he answered.

She said, "Do you think God would make spring come just for one boy who's mad at him? God doesn't work that way. He doesn't interfere in the world all the time. He set many things running and he watches and protects them. But he doesn't change things just for little boys who are mad. Would you want God to work like that?"

He took off his overshoes and didn't look up and didn't answer.

When spring came and the birds hung the branches down, not the next day and not on bargain day, but on a day he scarcely noticed, it was there. And he scuttled into the house and said, "I've made a new bargain."

His mother frowned, "What?"

"To thank God every time the grass sprouts."

The Wise May Bring Their Learning

Edward John Hopkins

The wise may bring their learning,
The rich may bring their wealth,
And some may bring their greatness,
And some bring strength and health;
We, too, would bring our treasures
To offer to the King;
We have no wealth or learning:
What shall we children bring?

We'll bring him hearts that love him;
We'll bring him thankful praise,
And young souls meekly striving
To walk in holy ways;

And these shall be the treasures
We offer to the king,
And these are gifts that even
The poorest child may bring.

We'll bring the little duties
We have to do each day;
We'll try our best to please him,
At home, at school, at play;
and better are these treasures
to offer to our King,
Than richest gifts without them;
Yet these a child may bring.

R. R. Bear

Marty Crisp

Sara smiled as mother painted a candy-pink stripe round and round her clumsy, white cast. This was to remind her that Christmas would soon be here. Sara knew that she wouldn't be home for Christmas. She'd be in the hospital with her broken leg. She tried not to think of Christmas.

She wiggled her toes as they hung above her, peeking out of her cast, suspended in traction so far away that she couldn't reach them to scratch.

"Mommy, itch my toes for me." Sara's voice was sad. Nothing mother did could really cheer her up. Nothing good could possibly happen when you were spending Christmas in the hospital.

"Sara," mother bent close, smoothing back Sara's long dark hair. "I have to go home to make dinner for dad and Tim, but I'll be back in a little while."

Sara reached up quickly, wrapping her arms around mother's neck. "Please don't go," she begged, "I'm scared when I'm alone."

Sara's mother kissed her and smiled. "The nurses are all here," she said "and just listen to that music!" Sara could hear a group of carolers singing "Joy to the World."

Sue, Sara's favorite nurse, appeared at the door with a pill, just as mother left the room.

"Please, Sue," Sara begged, "please stay and play a game with me. I don't want to be alone."

"I'll come back tonight, Sara, and read you a story, but I have to finish passing the medicine now." Sue quickly thumbed through the books stacked on Sara's bedside table. "How about 'The Night Before Christmas'? That sounds like a good story." She grinned at her from the door. "Hang in there, Sara, I'll be back soon."

Sara could feel her eyes filling with tears. One spilled over and began to slide down her cheek before she could wipe it away. *Why is everyone so busy?* she wondered.

Just then she heard a quiet knock at her door.

She turned her head slowly toward the door.

"May I come in?" A cheerful voice called. A young woman entered the room, carrying a large, brown bag. Sara sighed. She didn't want any more nut cups or apples. She didn't even want paper dolls or card games. There was nothing in the whole world she wanted that could fit in a brown paper bag.

"Hi! I'm Dottie Weber from Good Bears of the World." She came up beside the bed and rested her still-cold-from-the-outside hand on Sara's arm. "I'd like you to meet someone," she said, reaching into the bag.

"This is the Red Rose Bear." She pulled out a stuffed animal the size of a kitty cat. He was squeezably soft, covered with fuzzy, brown terry cloth skin. He had light blue, embroidered eyes and a flat, black felt nose. On his chest was a small, red rose. Sara didn't reach for him, although she wanted to.

"Did you know that Lancaster, Pennsylvania, is called the Red Rose city?" Sara nodded. Then Dottie said, "Some of us belong to a worldwide group called Good Bears. We call our group the Red Rose Group and so we call our bears R. R. Bears!" She laughed softly and rubbed the cuddly bear against Sara's cheek. "Our bears get lonely around Christmastime, so we find children who will love them." She paused. "This one's yours."

Sara Ann still hesitated. She didn't trust anybody tonight.

Dottie pulled another bear from the bag. It was an older bear, black with a brown muzzle. "This is Margaret," Dottie whispered in Sara's ear. "She likes to help me give out the bears."

"Whose teddy bear is she?" asked Sara.

"Why, she's mine!" Dottie grinned. "She's been with me for years."

Sara looked closely at Dottie and her bear. Maybe she was joking. But she looked like she meant what she was saying.

"Why would you have a teddy bear?" Sara asked suspiciously.

"Why?" Dottie sounded surprised. "Because she's my best friend. She's always around, always glad to listen, never interrupts me, never complains, and besides," Dottie hugged the old bear tightly, "she's nice to hug!"

Sara reached out and stroked the Red Rose Bear. "You mean this bear is all mine?"

Dottie nodded solemnly.

"But I can't call her Red Rose Bear. That's not friendly." Sara picked up the bear and looked carefully at its comfortable face. "I think I'll call her Rosie."

When Dottie left, with Margaret tucked under her arm, she stopped at the door to wave. Sara and Rosie were nestled together, and neither one looked lonely.

"I'm going to keep you forever," Sara spoke softly into the little bear's brown felt ear. "You'll never be lonely again."

The Tree That Trimmed Itself

Carolyn Sherwin Bailey

I wish, oh, how I wish!" sighed the young Pine Tree, as Christmas wind blew through its branches, "that I might be a Christmas Tree with decorations like my brother who was cut down!"

The forest was very still and cold. It was Christmas Eve, the season of wonder, but very few trees had been cut for the children. So many tall, strong ones would be needed for building homes and for kindling fires and for making furniture. But, oh, the happiness of a Christmas tree sparkling in the light of the home fire, with a circle of happy children dancing about it! No wonder that the young Pine Tree sighed again in the wind.

"I wish that I might be trimmed for Christmas!" it whispered.

Suddenly something happened there in the woods. Floating down among the outspread branches of the Pine Tree came white stars, shaped like shining crystals.

More and then still more snow stars fell, until every twig of every branch of the tree held its white star.

They were more beautiful than any ornaments that the toyman had for trimming a Christmas Tree.

But still the young Pine Tree longed for all the honors his brother tree would have. "I wish that I might hear the Christmas chimes!" it sighed in the wind.

Then the night grew colder and colder. The frost came through the forest and stopped beside the Pine Tree, hanging sharp, hard icicles to the tips of the twigs.

Whenever the wind touched the tree the icicles tinkled and rang like a chime of tiny Christmas bells. They made soft, beautiful Christmas music.

But still the young Pine Tree was not satisfied. "I wish," it sighed, "that I might hold lights as my brother will on this Christmas Eve."

Suddenly the stars shone out in the darkness and dropped their beams of light down as far as the branches of the young Pine Tree. One star seemed to leave the sky and rest on the top-most twig of the Pine Tree. There it flamed and flashed like a beacon to call everyone to see the wonders of Christmas Eve. The Pine Tree was lighted as brightly as if it carried a hundred candles, but still it had a wish.

"I am still not yet a Christmas Tree!" it sighed. "I wish that I might hold gifts among my branches." And it seemed as this wish could never come true, for where could Christmas gifts be found in the wintry forest?

Christmas Eve changed to the very early dawning of Christmas Day. Still the Pine Tree wore its snow stars. Its icicle chimes rang in the clear, cold air, and the light of the sky shone in its branches like a Christmas light. And out from the shelter of a nest among its roots crept a tiny mouse, cold and hungry.

How nice! Hanging to the Pine Tree, just above the nest of the mouse, was a bunch of berries and its trailing vine.

The vine had twisted itself around the trunk of the Tree in the summertime and now, in the deep winter, its bright berries hung there, a gift on Christmas morning for the hungry little mouse.

And out from the shelter of the trunk of the Pine Tree came a squirrel. He, too, was hungry. But he scampered along the branch until he came to the part of the Tree where it had held tightly, in spite of the winter gales, a fat, brown cone.

The squirrel held the cone daintily in his paws, cut out the seeds and munched them.

It was his holiday breakfast and how good it tasted! No better Christmas gift could have come to the squirrel than that fat pine cone so full of seeds.

"Merry Christmas!" called the children, running to the woods later on the morning of Christmas Day. "Merry Christmas, little Pine Tree. We have brought a gift for your snow bird. We heard him calling yesterday."

In their red caps and mittens, the happy children came dancing through the woods with a bundle of ripe grain.

They reached up as far as they could and hung it by a gay red ribbon to one of the green branches of the little Pine Tree. Then they exclaimed, and they stood farther back in the path, for the snow bird came out from an empty nest among the branches which grew thickest to feast on the grain.

"The snow bird rested in a cradle on Christmas Eve!" The children said to each other. "The little Pine Tree must have held that empty nest very closely all winter to give the snow bird a Christmas cradle!"

And the little Pine Tree stood straight and happy there in the woods on Christmas morning, for all of its wishes had come true. It had trimmed itself with stars and heard the chimes and had offered its gifts to its little neighbors of the forest. And still it could grow for the building of homes when it was an older, larger pine!

Company for Christmas   Alan Cliburn

Jason looked at his presents under the Christmas tree. Of all the gifts he had received, he liked the red roller skates best.

"Can I show my new skates to my friends?" he asked his father.

"Yes, but be careful," Mr. Allington replied. "The sidewalks are still slippery."

"And don't be gone too long," his mother added from the kitchen. "We're having company for Christmas dinner, you know. Be back in an hour."

Jason frowned. "How will I know when it's been an hour?".

Mr. Allington looked at his watch. "It's nearly 9:00 now. At 10:00 you'll hear the chimes in the church steeple. OK?"

"OK," Jason agreed.

He walked outside and sat down on the steps to put on his skates. The air was crisp and cool and patches of snow were everywhere. Mr. and Mrs. Hansen from next door passed on their way home from church.

"Merry Christmas!" Jason called out.

"Well, Merry Christmas to you, Jason," Mr. Hansen replied.

"Are those your new Christmas skates?" Mrs. Hansen asked.

"Yes," Jason said. "It's my most favorite present."

"Be sure and wish your parents a Merry Christmas for us," Mr. Hansen requested.

"I'll do it later," Jason decided. "I'm not allowed to wear my skates inside the house."

A moment later he was skating down the sidewalk. His friend Troy lived in the white house near the corner, but no one came to the door when he knocked.

"I believe they went away for the holiday," the woman in the next house told Jason when she came out to sweep the walk. "It is Christmas, after all."

"I wanted to show Troy my skates," Jason said.

"They're very nice, I'm sure," the woman answered. Then she went back inside.

It was the same everywhere Jason went. His friends had all gone away for Christmas. Finally Jason came to the park at the end of the block. Maybe his special friend would be there. But probably not, Jason thought. Not on Christmas.

"Hello, Jason," a voice said suddenly.

"Hi, Andy!" Jason exclaimed. "I didn't think you'd be here today. All my other friends went away for Christmas."

The old man shook his head. "Not me. No place to go! Besides, the pigeons expect me this time every day, and they don't understand about holidays."

"See my new skates?" Jason asked, sitting down next to Andy on the park bench. "They're red!"

"So they are," the old man agreed with a chuckle. "Couldn't be much redder than that!"

"What'd you get for Christmas?" Jason wanted to know.

Andy looked at him. "I got some very special gifts. Another day here in the park where I can enjoy the scenery and feed the birds, good health—considering I'm no spring chicken anymore—and friends like you, Jason."

"But what presents did you get?" Jason asked. "What was under your Christmas tree this morning?"

"All these trees in the park are my Christmas trees," Andy replied with a smile. "Didn't see any reason to put one inside my house."

"Ours has lights and tinsel and all kinds of decorations," Jason said. "Want to see me skate?"

"That would be very nice," Andy agreed. "Just watch out for that patch of ice over there."

Jason skated all over the park, coming back to Andy and doing some fancy spins.

"You're a good skater," Andy told him, nodding his head.

Suddenly church chimes filled the air with their music. "It's 10:00!" Jason exclaimed.

"So it is," Andy replied, pulling a gold watch out of his pocket.

"I have to go home," Jason continued. "We're having company for Christmas dinner."

"Well, thank you for spending part of Christmas with me," Andy said. "Probably see you tomorrow."

"I'll be here," Jason promised. "Where will you be going for Christmas dinner, Andy?"

"Me?" the old man answered. "I don't guess I'll be going anywhere."

"But won't you be with your family?" Jason questioned. "You're supposed to be with your family on Christmas. My aunt and uncle and cousins are coming, plus a neighbor up the block."

"My family doesn't live around here," Andy explained. "You'd better hurry on home now or you'll be late. Merry Christmas, Jason."

"Merry Christmas," Jason echoed, skating toward home.

His father was getting the big table ready when Jason entered the house. "Just in time to help me with the chairs," Mr. Allington said.

"OK," Jason agreed, putting his skates in their box under the tree.

"Set one less place than we planned on," Mrs. Allington called from the kitchen.

"Why?" Jason wanted to know. "Who's sick?"

"Nobody's sick," his mother replied, coming to the door with a big spoon in her hand. "Our neighbor, Mrs. Collins, had a chance to go to her daughter's house after all, so she won't be with us. We'll have nine for dinner instead of ten."

"Could I invite Andy?" Jason asked suddenly. "He doesn't eat very much."

His parents looked at him. "Andy?" Mr. Allington repeated. "Who's Andy?"

"A friend of mine," Jason said. "And he doesn't have any place to go for Christmas dinner."

His mother frowned. "A friend of yours? And he doesn't have any place to go for Christmas? Surely he must have a family!"

"No, he lives by himself in an old house by the park," Jason explained. "His family isn't around here."

"Do you mean that old man who feeds the pigeons?" Mr. Allington wanted to know.

"Yes, that's Andy!" Jason agreed. "Can we invite him? Please!"

His parents were silent for a moment. "We don't even know him," Mr. Allington began finally.

"He probably has plans," Mrs. Allington added.

"But *I* know him," Jason reminded them. "And he doesn't have any plans at all!"

"Jason, you don't understand," his father said.

"I understood what the pastor was saying in church last night," Jason replied. "He said Christmas is a time for remembering the special love God had for us when he sent Jesus, and we should show we remember by loving others—something like that."

His mother swallowed. "That was exactly what he said." She looked at Jason's father. "What do you think?"

Mr. Allington grinned. "What are we waiting for? Let's go get Andy before somebody else does!"

An hour later 10 people were sitting around the Allington table, eating turkey and having a wonderful time.

"This is just about the best Christmas I've ever had," Andy said. "I sure do thank you folks for inviting me."

"We're just glad you could share it with us, Andy," Mr. Allington told him. "Right, Jason?"

"Right," Jason agreed, smiling at his friend. "And after dinner I'll even let Andy try out my new skates!"

"Thank you kindly," Andy replied, "but I'll settle for a second piece of pumpkin pie instead!"

Everybody laughed. Especially Jason. It was a neat Christmas.

A Christmas Carol

Gilbert Keith Chesterton

The Christ child lay on Mary's lap,
His hair was like a light.
(O weary, weary were the world,
But here is all aright.)

The Christ child lay on Mary's breast,
His hair was like a star.
(O stern and cunning are the kings,
But here the true hearts are.)

The Christ child lay on Mary's heart,
His hair was like a fire.
(O weary, weary is the world,
But here the world's desire.)

The Christ child stood at Mary's knee,
His hair was like a crown,
And all the flowers looked up at him,
And all the stars looked down.

How a Mouse Changed Christmas

Alice Cameron Bostrom

Franz Gruber shook the snow from his dark hair as he entered the onion-towered church of St. Nikola in Austria. It was December 24, 1818. He had come to practice the organ for the midnight Christmas Eve service.

Franz sat down at the organ, pulled out the stops, pumped on the bellow pedals, and pressed the keys. Not a sound came out.

Franz turned as the assistant pastor came into the church. "Joseph," he said, "what is wrong with the organ?"

The two men climbed to the loft behind the organ pipes. Evidence of a mouse gave them their answer. During the night a hungry mouse had come to the loft and chewed on the leather bellows, which provided wind for the pipes of the organ. One small hole had silenced the mighty voice of the organ. And at Christmas!

Franz looked at Joseph. "Can the organ be fixed?" he asked.

"No, not until spring," Joseph said.

"But, Joseph, how can we have a Christmas Eve service without music?"

The two men stood in silence, wondering what to do.

Joseph, the young pastor, spoke a little shyly. "I have a poem, Franz."

"What good is a poem, Joseph?" Franz asked.

Joseph became excited as he answered. "You are a fine musician," he said. "You could write some music and play the guitar for the new song. The two of us could sing with the help of the children's choir."

"Let me see the poem, Joseph. I don't know if I can write the music in time for the midnight service," Franz said.

Joseph waited as Franz read the words. Joseph's excitement seemed to catch hold of Franz. He grabbed his hat and coat and hurried toward the church door. "I'll be back as quickly as I can!" he called. "But I don't know about the guitar. The people will not like a guitar in the church service."

Franz walked to Arnsdorf, the next town, where he was the schoolmaster. Back in his room above the school, Franz played the pianoforte (as the piano was called in those days). He tried different melodies to go with Joseph's words. Finally, he decided upon a simple melody which seemed to fit.

He took his guitar from the peg on the wall and hurried back to the church. There six boys and six girls, the very best from the church choir, stood waiting to learn the new Christmas song.

Franz and Joseph helped the children learn their parts while the two men practiced the harmony. The children forgot about the snow outside and the games they wanted to play. They felt warm and happy as they sang. A little mouse might have damaged the church organ, but the pastor, the organist, and the 12 boys and girls would turn the Christmas Eve service into a very special celebration of Jesus' birth.

Time for the service approached. Candles lit up the great church. Pine boughs, cut from nearby trees, added beauty and fragrance. Soon the worshipers entered the church and walked down the silent aisles. The people in bright scarves and woolen clothes looked at each other. Where was the organ music?

The senior pastor read some scripture passages. He finished by telling of Jesus' birth and closed the Bible.

Then a small group of children stepped forward. The girls had red and green ribbons tied to their braids. The boys had small pieces of ribbons attached to their stockings. The assistant pastor and the organist stepped forward.

"An accident happened to our organ last night," Joseph said. He waited until the murmuring stopped. "We have some new music for you however."

As the guitar strummed, Franz and Joseph began to sing a lullaby. The children sang the chorus of the new song, which would become the most famous Christmas song around the world: *Stille Nacht! Heilige Nacht!*—"Silent Night! Holy Night!"

After the service as the people moved slowly out into the snow, the assistant pastor and the organist shook hands.

"Merry Christmas, Joseph Mohr," Franz said.

"The same to you, Franz Gruber," Joseph answered. "Despite the hungry mouse, it is indeed a Merry Christmas."

"For Hungry Poeple"
Celia Lehman

Ten-year-old Teresa and her sister Kristi sat in the backseat of the family car on the way home from church. They were strapped in seat belts and for once sat quietly. They were listening to mom and dad talking about Pastor Bill's sermon.

"Maybe we shouldn't give each other Christmas presents this year. We should take that money and give it to those hungry people," mom said.

"No presents?" gasped Kristi who was one year younger than Teresa. There were always presents under the tree before. Why, it just wouldn't be Christmas without presents.

Now dad was talking. "What you're saying is fine and good but the girls would be disappointed."

Both girls were shaking their heads up and down.

Dad continued. "Maybe what we ought to do is get presents for the girls but not get presents for each other." He gave mom a quick glance and kept driving. Soon they were back home.

Teresa ran directly to her room. She took off her coat, laid her Bible on the dresser, and sat at the edge of the bed. She was thinking what to do if mom and dad decided not to get any presents.

Soon she smelled hamburgers frying. *I wonder what it would feel like not to have yummie hamburgers and fried potatoes and fresh salad?* Oh, she'd be very glad to let some boy or girl have the peas but certainly not the cake and ice cream mom had planned for dessert.

But the pastor said that some children were dying because they hadn't eaten anything for days and days, she thought to herself. Now she remembered the orange juice she had for breakfast and the cinnamon toast and a sunny-side-up egg mom had fried for her. The thought of it made her stomach growl.

Suddenly she had an idea. She knew what she would do—

When mom went to wash the dishes she saw an envelope by the microwave oven.

"What's all this about?" she said to the girls who were drying the dishes. Kristi looked at Teresa. Teresa looked down.

"Teresa, did you put this envelope here?"

Mom turned the envelope around and read, "For hungry poeple."

Teresa blurted out, "I gave them everything I had, mom. It's for those hungry people. I gave it all."

Kristi crowded closer to take a look. "You spelled *people* wrong."

"Oh, Teresa!" exclaimed mom as she gave Teresa a big hug. "Everyone knows what you mean. If everyone who ate dinner today would take all the money they had in their banks, how happy those hungry people would be to have something to eat."

Suddenly Kristi didn't want to be left out. She dashed up the stairs. Quick as a flash she was back.

"Here's all I got, mom. They can have mine, too."

Dad ducked his head through the kitchen door. "What's all the excitement about out here?" he wanted to know.

Mom showed the envelope to dad. Together they counted the money. Teresa had $4.00 in her envelope. Kristi had $6.00.

"What should we do with it?" mom asked.

"We could send it to our church's world hunger committee. They'd make sure the food got to India or Africa or anyplace where people are hungry," replied dad.

Mom continued, "With $10.00 some family can buy a loaf of bread, a half gallon of milk, some eggs, a few bananas, and some peas," she said.

Everyone laughed and looked at Teresa.

"You can forget the peas," scowled Teresa. "I hope those parents will buy their little girl some ice cream instead."

The Practical Gift

Phyliss Doudna

Dad had a new job at the Smith Dairy. Mom said this was the nicest Christmas present the family could have, because dad had been out of work for six months. Mom also told Bobby that Christmas presents would have to be *practical* this year because they didn't have money for toys.

When Bobby opened his packages on Christmas morning, he found a new comb, a pair of pajamas, and a big, shiny flashlight.

"I've never had a flashlight," he said.

His mother smiled. "We think you need one to have by your bed at night."

Bobby turned it on, but it didn't seem to make much light.

"It will work better in the dark. Go into the closet to try it," his father suggested.

Bobby did this. He called his mom and dad to see how bright a light it made. Then Bobby got out some coloring books and toys to play with. He was happy. Mom was preparing a good Christmas dinner. After that, they were going to visit his cousins.

"May I take my flashlight with me, mom?" he asked.

"Sure, you can show it to Paula and Bret," his mother replied.

Rain was pouring down by the time they left. It took an hour to get there. The relatives greeted each other with "Merry Christmas!"

"Look what I got," Bobby said, excitedly holding up his flashlight.

"That's nice," his cousin Bret replied. "Come see my presents."

Bret led him to a corner full of toys. There was an electric train set on a track with regular railroad crossing signs. There was a computer.

Paula showed Bobby her new doll with three different outfits of clothes. She also had a small ironing board and an electric iron.

Suddenly Bobby felt funny inside. These were nice toys. He wished he had received something like them. No one had taken much notice of his flashlight. Maybe it wasn't such a nice present after all.

"It looks as though we're in for a real storm," Uncle Ben said. Lightning, which could be seen through the windows, was quickly followed by the deep rumble of thunder.

Suddenly the lights went out. All was dark except for occasional lightning flashes.

"Ruth, where are the candles?" Uncle Ben asked.

"In the chest in our bedroom," Aunt Ruth answered.

"Not an easy place to see at a time like this. I wish we had a flashlight."

"Here's mine." Bobby felt his way to where Uncle Ben was sitting.

"Thanks, Bobby." The flashlight's strong beam lighted the room when his uncle turned it on. "That's better. Bobby, come with me to hold the light. Everyone else stay where you are while we find the candles."

They soon returned, and within a few minutes the room was fairly well lighted.

"How about some fruit juice and cookies?" Aunt Ruth suggested. "We can enjoy them while the electricity is off." As she started toward the kitchen, she turned. "Bobby, could I use your flashlight? Better yet, will you hold it for me while I work?"

That is just what he did. For the next hour, before the lights came on, his gift was in constant use.

"The storm has calmed down, so we'd better be going," dad said. "Bobby, don't forget your flashlight."

"I won't. We might need it if you have to change a tire."

"For goodness sake, don't say that," dad said. "Not in this weather anyhow."

"This really has been a Merry Christmas," Bobby said as he lay down in the backseat of the car. "Thanks for giving me a practical gift!"

Christmas Is Remembering

Elsie Binns

Christmas is remembering
Shy shepherds on a hill
And voices echoing
"Peace—Good will!"

Christmas is remembering
A stable and a star
And wise men journeying
From afar.

Christmas is remembering
A newborn baby boy
And all the world caroling
Songs of joy.

The Wooden Shoes of Little Hans

A European Legend   **Retold by Ron and Lyn Klug**

Once, long ago in a land across the sea, there lived a little boy, just eight years old, named Hans. He was an orphan and lived with his aunt, a mean, selfish, old woman who never tucked him in bed at night or gave him a kiss. "You are good for nothing! All you do is eat!" she would say as she reluctantly handed him a bowl of watery soup.

Because the aunt owned her own house and because everyone in the town knew she had a stocking full of gold hidden away, she did not dare send Hans to the school for poor children. She had to send him to the school with the rich children, but by wheedling and complaining she managed to get the schoolmaster to lower his price.

The schoolmaster was a kind man, but he could not protect Hans from the other boys, who made fun of Hans for his ragged clothes and forced him to run errands for them. Hans was so miserable that he often hid where no one could see him and cried until his eyes were red.

He was especially sad at Christmastime. Every Christmas the schoolmaster had the boys gather at the school. Then he marched them all to the church for the evening service. After that, the boys returned to their own houses to celebrate Christmas with their families.

This year the winter was especially hard. Cold winds had blown for days, and snow lay thick on the ground. The pupils who gathered at the school wore new jackets, fur-lined caps, and warm boots—all except for little Hans, who stood shivering in his tattered everyday clothes and his wooden shoes.

"Look at the orphan!" one of the biggest boys exclaimed. "And see those wooden shoes!" All the other boys laughed, but Hans paid little attention because he was too busy blowing on his hands and stamping his feet to keep them warm.

When all the boys had arrived, they marched behind the schoolmaster to the church. Inside, it was warmer, and the candles glowed with a gentle light. Sitting in one corner by himself, Hans was almost happy.

While waiting for the church service to begin, the boys began to boast about the Christmas celebrations they would have at home later that night.

"We will have the biggest and finest goose in town," boasted the mayor's son.

"We will have the tallest Christmas tree, covered with oranges and sugar plums," said another boy.

Then all the boys began to talk about the wonderful gifts that would be in their shoes, which they would place carefully by the fireplace before they went to bed.

"Candy!" said one.

"Warm mittens!" said another.

"New toys!" they all said.

Hans listened to the other boys, knowing all he would get from his selfish aunt was a trip to bed without any supper. But because he had been good all year, he still hoped that the Christ child would not forget him, so he planned to put his wooden shoes in front of the fireplace.

When the Christmas Eve service was over, the boys burst out of the church, eager to enjoy the treats waiting for them at home.

Near the door of the church, on a stone bench tucked into an archway, lay a child asleep. He was dressed in a white robe. Beside him on the ground, tied in a cloth, were a hammer, a chisel, and a saw—the tools of a carpenter's apprentice. Under the light of the stars, his soft, curling blond hair seemed to glow. On this dark winter night his bare feet, sticking out from under his robe, were blue with cold.

The school boys in their warm coats and sturdy boots passed by the unknown child without a glance. Only little Hans, the last to leave the church, stopped to look at the sleeping boy.

"How terrible!" Hans said to himself. "This poor child has no stockings to wear in this cold weather. Even worse, he has no shoes to leave beside him while he sleeps so that the Christ child can leave him a gift."

Hans was so sad that he took off the wooden shoe from his right foot and placed it on the ground beside the sleeping child. Then, as well as he could, he hopped and limped his way home through the snow.

"You good for nothing!" cried his aunt when Hans returned home. "What have you done with your shoe?"

Hans thought of lying and saying that he had lost it, but instead, shivering with fear, he told her the truth about the barefoot boy beside the church.

"What a fool you are!" his aunt cried. "To spoil a pair of shoes for a beggar! Well, I will put the shoe that is left by the fireplace, and tonight the Christ child will leave a stick to beat you with when you awake. And tomorrow you will have nothing to eat but bread and water. This will teach you to give your shoe to the first beggar you see."

With that, she boxed Hans's ears and sent him to sleep in the cold attic. There the heart-broken boy lay in the darkness, crying himself to sleep.

In the morning, as Hans lay huddled in the attic, he heard his aunt cry out in surprise. He hurried downstairs and saw her standing open-mouthed and trembling.

Before the fireplace was a great heap of bright toys, boxes of candy, piles of fruit. And there in front of all the treasures was the wooden shoe he had given to the sleeping boy by the church. Next to it was his other shoe, which his aunt had placed there, expecting to put in it a stick with which to beat him.

As Hans stood wide-eyed before the gifts, he heard excited shouts from the street. He ran out and right into the arms of the schoolmaster.

"Hans, have you heard?" the kindly man asked. "All the children of the rich, who were expecting splendid gifts, found only sticks in their shoes! And what is even more strange, this morning, above the bench near the church door, the pastor found a golden circle formed in the old stones."

And so all the people knew that the boy sleeping next to the carpenter's tools was the Christ child himself, and he had rewarded the goodness of little Hans.

The Boy Who Hated Christmas

Robert C. Gremmels

*I*t was the day before Christmas, and everyone at Tommy's house was happy—everyone, that is, except Tommy.

Out in the kitchen Tommy's mother and his sister Carol were making Christmas cookies. Tommy's father was busy cracking Christmas nuts.

Tommy could hear them humming little Christmas songs as they worked.

But Tommy wasn't humming. He wasn't even in the kitchen. He was in the living room, looking at the Christmas tree. And he was angry.

Tommy hated Christmas cookies. And he hated Christmas nuts. And he hated Christmas trees. He even hated to see his father and his mother and his sister Carol so happy with the Christmas spirit. Tommy hated these things because Tommy hated Christmas itself.

Tommy looked down at all the lovely gifts that had been placed around the tree. He hated them, too. He knew all the *nice* presents would be for Carol. She always got all the nice things, he thought. Because she was a *girl!*

For a long time Tommy stood in front of the tree. Thinking. Why didn't *he* get presents as nice as Carol's? "She always gets the nice things," he said to himself. "All I ever get is a ball, or a train, or a shovel." Tommy thought he knew why. "They like her better than they like me," he said.

Suddenly Tommy had an idea. "If I give a real nice present to mom and dad," he thought, "maybe they'll like *me* better. And then *I'll* get the nice things. Tommy thought about this for a while. Then he smiled—for the first time all day.

Quickly Tommy ran to his bedroom and took out the piggy bank from his dresser drawer. He shook it very hard. There were a lot of pennies in it. Enough to buy the best present he could think of—a big box of candy, like the one he had seen at the store down at the corner.

Tommy ran to the kitchen. "Mom," he cried, "can I take the pennies out of my bank?"

"Why, Tommy," she answered, "you know you can. Don't you remember what we told you? Every year on the day before Christmas you can take out as many pennies as you want in order to buy presents."

"I know, mom," Tommy said. "But I've never taken them out before. I've never bought any presents before."

"Well, you take as many as you need," his mother said.

"And can I go to the store?" Tommy asked.

"If you want to, Tommy," she said.

Quickly Tommy ran back to his room. He opened his bank and began to count the pennies. One, two, three . . . 87, 88 . . . 163. . . . At last he had counted 375—enough to buy the box of candy.

Tommy counted out an extra penny, just in case he should lose one on the way. Then he ran as fast as he could to the store. And he bought the biggest, reddest box of candy you ever saw.

As soon as the store clerk had wrapped the candy in a pretty Christmas wrapping, Tommy clutched it tightly and ran home again. Quietly

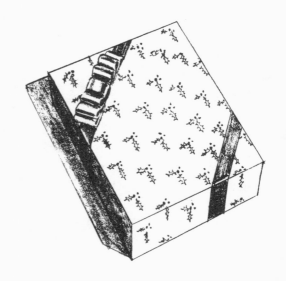

he crept into the house and placed the present neatly beside the other gifts under the tree. Then he went to the kitchen to help his father crack nuts.

On Christmas Day Tommy was very happy. After church Tommy and his mother and his father and his sister Carol all gathered around the Christmas tree to open their gifts.

Tommy could hardly wait until mom and dad opened the gift he had bought for them. He hardly seemed to notice when Carol opened one of her packages and found a bright new dress. Or when she opened another and found a big doll that rolled its eyes and cried real tears.

"Mom!" Tommy called out. "Open the present I bought!" He could hardly sit still.

"All right, Tommy," she said. She picked up the package and began to unwrap it. As the last piece of wrapping came off, Tommy let out a scream of joy.

"Why, Tommy," his mother said. "What a beautiful box of candy!"

And Tommy's father looked at him very kindly and said, "Thank you, Tommy. Thank you very much."

And Tommy was happier than he had ever been before. He ran to mom and dad and kissed them. He hadn't opened his presents yet, but he knew they would be every bit as nice as Carol's.

"You know, mom," Tommy said, "Christmas is a lot more fun when you give presents instead of just getting them."

And Tommy knew he would never hate Christmas again.

Paul's After-Christmas Party

Florence J. Johnson

Paul's birthday came in January, right after New Year's Day. He wanted a party because it wouldn't be a birthday without one. But there had been so many parties during the Christmas holidays, and Nancy Lee had had a birthday party just a few days before Christmas.

Paul wished he could think of something different—a birthday party that wouldn't be the same old games with cake and ice cream.

He looked at the big Christmas tree in the living room. The needles were falling, and it wasn't bright green any longer. Mother had said that they would have to take it down. They would do as they did last year, put it out on the lawn and make it a feeding station for the birds. It was fun decorating it outside.

Paul looked at the tree with new interest. There was the answer to his problem. He would help his mother take off all the ornaments and the tinsel and have it ready to be redecorated when the guests came.

Paul was busy. There were many things to do to be ready for the party.

Saturday afternoon came. The Christmas tree was standing on the side lawn looking lonely and forlorn with no sparkling ornaments to catch the bright, winter sunshine. There were only a few straggling silver icicles hanging on the bare branches.

"What kind of games are we going to play?" asked Donna when all the guests had arrived.

"It's going to be a funny kind of a party," laughed Paul as he came from the kitchen. He was carrying a big pan of popcorn and a pincushion which held several big needles already threaded with coarse, heavy thread. "First thing we do is make popcorn strings," he said.

"Why?" Steve wanted to know. "Christmas is past. We don't trim trees now."

"Just wait and see."

Betty Ann took a needle and a handful of popcorn. She had done this many times. But, why did Paul want to do it after Christmas? Besides, they had taken their tree down. She looked out of the window. And there was Paul's Christmas tree out in the yard with a few birds fluttering about the empty branches.

Betty Ann jumped up, spilling her popcorn all over the floor, and laughed aloud.

"I know what we are going to do. We are trimming a tree for the birds. And look, they're already waiting for us."

Everyone came running to the window. Sure enough, there were birds flying around. A squirrel who had not saved up enough winter supplies was sitting nearby, and a little gray rabbit was hopping about in the snow.

Now fingers flew faster. It wasn't long before the popcorn was all strung. Then Paul brought out several orange cups—orange halves that had been shellacked so they would last longer. These were filled with different kinds of seeds. Next, some pieces of suet were tied with the string; then bright-red apples were cut in quarters and also tied with string.

"It's going to be a beautiful tree," said Donna when everything was ready, and they were putting on their wraps to go out and trim the tree.

What fun it was to drape the strings of popcorn through the branches and to fasten the orange cups, the suet, and the red apples! The little birds kept fluttering about as if they knew they were to have a part in this different birthday party. A squirrel chattered in the big tree, and a little gray rabbit watched from the hedge.

After the tree was trimmed, the boys and the girls ran into the house to warm their tingling fingers and toes. Besides, it was time for the birthday treat.

In the center of the table was the big birthday cake with seven green candles.

At each place was a big popcorn ball in which had been fastened a tiny Christmas tree candle.

How good those big bowls of hot soup tasted with lots of crunchy crackers! And then came the dessert—a birthday cake and pink and green ice cream!

Every now and then someone would jump up and run to the window to see how many more birds had come to their Christmas tree.

"There are two squirrels there and three rabbits now," said Steve. "They sure are enjoying those nuts and carrots."

"This has been the nicest party," said Donna happily.

"It's lots more fun doing something different!" said Betty Ann.

"Three cheers to Paul for his after-Christmas party!" exclaimed Steve.

Winds through the Olive Trees

Katherine Parker

Winds through the olive trees
Softly did blow
Round little Bethlehem
Long, long ago.

Sheep on the hillside lay
Whiter than snow.
Shepherds were watching them,
Long, long ago.

Then from the happy skies
Angels bent low,
Singing their songs of joy,
Long, long ago.

For in a manger bed,
Cradled, we know,
Christ came to Bethlehem,
Long, long ago.

A Bell Cookie

Elizabeth Phillips

*I*t was a happy time for Nita. It was a happy time for everyone in Nita's family. It was Christmastime. Nita and her big brother Dale were wrapping presents. There were pieces of paper and ribbon scattered about on the table.

"I love surprises, don't you?" Nita smiled at her brother Dale.

"Sure!" Dale answered. "I'm all finished wrapping my presents." He gathered his packages up and placed them under the tree. "Aren't you finished yet?" he asked.

"Almost," she answered. "I have to wrap the cookies for my teacher and my classmates. I have a present for everyone in my room. Mom made some cookies shaped like Christmas trees, except one. It's shaped like a big fat bell. I decorated the cookies with candy decorations. Now I can give

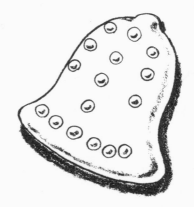

everyone a cookie. Aren't they beautiful? They are too pretty to eat."

Mother laughed as she came into the room. "Let's count them and make sure that we have enough."

Nita set aside the bell-shaped cookie. "That one is for Miss Campbell," she explained. Then she counted. There were 25 Christmas cookies. She put aside one of them. "I don't need this one."

"But I thought there were 25 children in your class," mother said.

"There are," Nita nodded. "But I'm not going to give Ginger one."

"But, Nita, you can't leave Ginger out," mother protested.

Nita frowned. "But I don't like Ginger. She pushes and shoves and always wants to be first."

Mother sat down beside Nita. "You may not like the way Ginger plays, but it makes me unhappy to hear you say that you don't like someone."

Nita squirmed in her chair. "OK, I'll give Ginger a cookie too." Then she got busy wrapping the cookies. She wrapped each in tissue paper and tied it with a ribbon. She wrapped Miss Campbell's cookie in the prettiest paper she could find. Then she fastened on a fluffy, red bow. She didn't bother to put a bow on Ginger's cookie—not even a ribbon. She sealed the tissue with a piece of Christmas Scotch tape.

The next day Nita got up early and dressed. This was the day for the Christmas party at school. Each one in the class had drawn a name for giving a present. She had that gift ready too. She put all the gifts in a big bag. Ginger's cookie went in first.

I don't care if it gets mashed a little, she thought. On top of all the other gifts she placed the one for Miss Campbell.

When it was time to give out the gifts, Miss Campbell chose Nita to give them out. Nita walked up and down the aisles giving out the presents.

Miss Campbell's desk was piled high with presents. Nita decided she would give her gift to the teacher at the very last. She looked over at Ginger. Ginger sat very still. Some of the children had two or three or even more gifts on their desks, but Ginger had only one little one. Nita knew it was from the person who had drawn Ginger's name.

Nita walked down the aisle slowly. Ginger looked sad. Nita knew that when Ginger saw her plainly wrapped cookie she would be even sadder.

Maybe I should give her the special bell cookie. But then I would have to give Miss Campbell the ugly one, Nita thought.

Everyone laughed and showed one another their gifts. Everyone but Ginger. She looked as if she were going to cry any minute.

Nita thought how terrible it must be not to have any friends. She wondered how she would feel. Then, she knew exactly what to do!

She hurried to Ginger's desk. She put her hand in the bag and felt the big, red bow on the bell cookie. Nita pulled it out carefully and put it on Ginger's desk. As she walked on to the front of the room, she turned and saw Ginger's face. It had the biggest, surprised smile she had ever seen.

Again the girl felt in the bag. She pulled out the present from the bottom of the bag. She had wanted her teacher's present to be special, but now she had to give her one without a ribbon and a bow. Somehow the paper had even got torn. Nita felt ashamed to put it on the desk by the others. She laid it down and turned quickly away.

But Miss Campbell caught her arm. "Thank you for this gift, and thank you for the other one too!"

Nita looked at the teacher.

The teacher whispered in her ear, "I saw what you did. Your kindness to Ginger was the best gift you could give me." She smiled.

After a moment Nita smiled too.

In The Great Walled Country

Raymond MacDonald Alden

Away at the northern end of the world, where most people suppose that there is nothing but ice and snow, is a land full of children. It is called The Great Walled Country, because all around the country is a great wall of ice, hundreds of feet thick and hundreds of feet high.

Nobody who lives there ever grows up. The king and the queen, the princes and the courtiers, play a great deal of the time with dolls and tin soldiers. Every night at seven o'clock they have a bowl of bread and milk and go to bed. But they make excellent rulers, and the other children are well pleased with the government.

In The Great Walled Country, they never have to buy their Christmas presents. Every year, on the day before Christmas, Grandfather Christmas (I suppose we would call him Santa Claus) goes into a great forest of Christmas trees that grows just back of the palace of the king. There he fills the trees with candy and books and toys and all sorts of good things. When night comes, all the children wrap up snugly and go to the forest to gather gifts for their friends. Each one goes by himself so that none of his friends can see what he has gathered. And no one ever thinks of such a thing as taking a present for himself.

So Christmas time is a great holiday in that land. They have been celebrating it in this way for hundreds of years.

But there was once a time, many years ago, when the children in The Great Walled Country had a very strange Christmas. There came a visitor to the land. He was an old man, and he was the first stranger for many years who had succeeded in getting over the wall.

The stranger looked so wise that the king invited him to the palace.

When this old man was told how they held their Christmas celebration, he listened gravely. Then, looking wiser than ever, he said to the king, "That is all very well, but I should think there would be an easier way. Why does not everyone get his own presents? That would save the trouble of dividing them again, and everyone would be better satisfied. He could pick out just what he wanted for himself."

This seemed to the king a very wise saying. He called all his courtiers and counselors about him, and they all agreed they had been very foolish. "We will make a proclamation," they said, "and always after this follow the new plan."

So the proclamation was made. The plan seemed as wise to the children of the country as it had to the king and the counselors. Everyone had at some time been a little disappointed with his Christmas gifts; now there would be no danger of that.

On Christmas Eve, they always had a meeting at the palace and sang carols until ten o'clock, the time for going to the forest. On this particular night, it seemed to the king that the music was not quite so merry as usual, and that the children's eyes did not shine as gladly as in other years. But there could be no good reason for this, since everyone was expecting a better time than usual. So he thought no more of it.

There was only one person at the palace that night who was not pleased with the new proclamation about the Christmas gifts. This was a little boy named Inge, who lived with his sister. Now his sister was unable to walk, and had to sit all day looking out of the window from her chair. Inge had always gone to the forest on Christmas Eve and returned with his arms and pockets loaded with pretty things for his sister, which would keep her amused all the coming year.

Now, said Inge to himself, what would his sister do? The poor child could not go a step toward the forest. After thinking about it a long time, Inge silently made up his mind not to obey the proclamation. He decided that it would not be wrong if, instead of taking gifts for himself, he took them altogether for his sister.

And now the chimes had struck ten. The children were making their way toward the forest in starlight so bright that it almost showed their shadows on the sparkling snow. As soon as they came to the edge of the forest they separated, each one going by himself in the old way. Though now there was really no reason why they should have secrets from one another.

Ten minutes later, if you had been in the forest you might have seen the children standing in dismay. For, as they looked eagerly about them, they saw

no presents hanging from the branches of the evergreen trees. High and low they searched, wandering farther into the forest than ever before. But still no presents appeared.

As the children were trooping out of the forest, after hours of weary searching, some of them came upon little Inge. Over his shoulder he was carrying a bag that seemed to be full to overflowing.

"Are they not beautiful things?" he cried. "I think Grandfather Christmas was never so good to us before."

"Why, what do you mean?" cried the children. "There are no presents in the forest."

"No presents!" said Inge. "I have my bag full of them." But he did not offer to show them, because he did not want the children to see that they were all for his little sister.

Then the children begged him to tell in what part of the forest he had found his presents. He turned back and pointed to the place where he had been. "I left many more behind than I brought away," he said. "There they are! I can see some of the things shining on the trees even from here."

But when the children followed his footprints in the snow, they still saw nothing on the trees. They thought that Inge must be dreaming.

On Christmas Day there was sadness all through The Great Walled Country. But those who came to the house of Inge and his sister saw plenty of books and dolls and beautiful toys piled up about the little girl's chair. When they asked where these things came from, they were told, "Why, from the Christmas-tree forest." And they shook their heads, not knowing what it could mean.

The king held a council in the palace. He appointed a committee to visit Grandfather Christmas and see what was the matter.

The committee set out upon their journey. They had very hard work to climb the great wall of ice that lay between their country and where Grandfather Christmas lived. But at last they found themselves in the very place where Grandfather Christmas lay sound asleep.

It was hard to waken him, for he always slept 100 days after his Christmas work was over. It was only by turning the hands of the clock around 200 times that the committee could do anything. But at last Grandfather Christmas sat up in bed, rubbing his eyes.

"Oh, sir!" cried the prince who was in charge of the committee. "We have come from the king of The Great Walled Country, to ask why you forgot us this Christmas and left no presents in the forest."

"No presents!" said Grandfather Christmas. "I never forget anything. The presents were there. You did not see them, that's all."

But the children told him that they had searched long and carefully.

"Indeed!" said Grandfather Christmas. "And did little Inge, the boy with the crippled sister, find none?"

Then the committee were silent. They had heard of the gifts at Inge's house, and did not know what to say.

"You had better go home," said Grandfather Christmas, "and let me finish my nap. The presents were there, but they were never intended for children who were looking only for themselves. I am not surprised that you could not see them. Remember that not everything wise travelers tell you is wise." And he turned over and went to sleep again.

The committee returned silently to The Great Walled Country, and told the king what they had heard. The next December, the king made another proclamation, bidding everyone to seek gifts for others, in the old way, in the Christmas-tree forest.

So that is what they have been doing ever since.

The Heart of Christmas

Dr. Bernhard M. Christensen

Some years ago I spent a winter teaching a rural school in a Polish community in Wisconsin. One of the outstanding events of the school year was the Christmas program, when all the parents and friends of the children were invited to come and hear them give their recitations and songs concerning the Christ child and Christmas. Of all the numbers that made up that evening's program, I remember especially the two short verses recited by a little chubby-faced, seven-year-old boy named Tony.

Tony's mother had left her husband and family and gone away to the city; so the four little boys were being brought up in various homes in the neighborhood. Perhaps this rather sad story connected with Tony's home helped to make me particularly interested in him.

I can still see his ruddy cheeks and deep brown eyes on the evening of the Christmas program when, dressed in his plain gray "waist," homemade knickers, long woolen stockings, and rubber boots, he stood up to "say his piece."

> *If I knew where to find him,*
> *The baby in the hay,*
> *I'd take a Christmas present*
> *To him this very day:*
> *Two little hands to serve him,*
> *And a loving heart to lift,*
> *And just myself on Christmas day*
> *To be his birthday gift.*

More than 20 years have gone by since then, and I have heard many sermons and speeches about the Christmas story. But none of them, it seems to me, has told more clearly or simply just what Christmas ought to mean to us, whether we are children or grown-ups, than did those few lines which little Tony spoke that evening in the Kirby Hills school.

Christmas teaches us the joy and blessedness of *giving*. "God so loved the world that he *gave* . . . ," says one of the most beautiful verses in our Bible. God gave his only Son to the world at the first Christmas, and through him God has given us not only all the good things of our life on earth but the forgiveness of our sins and everlasting life with him in heaven.

Jesus is God's Christmas present to the world. And surely it is right and good that we should celebrate his coming by giving gifts of all kinds to our relatives and friends, and especially to people who are in any kind of need or trouble. But our Christmas giving becomes poor and empty unless we have learned and acted on the deep yet simple truth expressed in little Tony's recitation:

> *. . . just myself, on Christmas Day,*
> *To be his birthday gift.*

We who have been brought up in the Christian church know that in order to give ourselves as a gift to the

Lord Jesus it is not necessary to find "the baby in the hay." For Jesus is near at hand in every home and in every heart that is open to him. Every one of us, the youngest child and the oldest man or woman, can speak to him in earnest prayer and tell him that we want to give ourselves to him and to belong to him forever. And all the treasures of the Wise Men, yes, all the gold and silver and precious stones of the whole world, do not mean as much to our Lord as a single heart given to him in childlike love and faith. For it was to win the love of our hearts that Jesus came to this earth and gave himself to us as the first and greatest of all Christmas gifts.

I wonder where little Tony is now. If he is still living, I am sure that he is no longer a little boy but a grown-up man with burdens to bear and problems to face in our great world filled with temptation and sin. Perhaps he has little boys of his own by now, ruddy-cheeked and starry-eyed as he himself used to be. I wonder if he has taught them the true meaning of Christmas giving, as he learned it long ago. If so, he has given to them the best of all gifts that a father or mother can give. For as the little children of our homes and schools and churches grow up into man- and womanhood, no gift could be more precious for them to receive than just to understand something of the wonderful message of Christmas: *that giving is the very heart of life*—giving ourselves to Christ, our Savior, and giving gifts of love and service to others in his name.

PRAYERS

Thanks for Jesus
Ron Klug

Sometimes, God, I can feel you are near me,
but I can't see you.
I'm glad that Jesus came to earth
to show us what you are like.
He helped people.
He healed the sick.
He fed the hungry.
He forgave people.
Thank you, God,
that Jesus came to live with us
and that he died and rose again
to show us your love for us
and your power over death.

A Prayer
Martin Luther

Ah, dearest Jesus, holy Child,
Make Thee a bed, soft, undefiled,
Within my heart, that it may be
A quiet chamber kept for Thee.

Prayer before Christmas
Pat Corrick Hinton

We are eager for your birthday, Lord Jesus.
We love the tinsel on the tree
and the decorations all around.
We love the making and the wrapping,
and we love the secrets under beds.
But most of all,
we love you, Lord.
We love you for loving us so much
that you wanted to be a human being
just like us.
Thank you for becoming a child
and showing us how to grow.
Come, Lord Jesus!
We are waiting for you.

Prayer at Christmas
Pat Corrick Hinton

God our Father,
it's Christmas at last.
Thank you for this big celebration.
We are happy because you have given us
your greatest gift of love,
Jesus your Son.
We welcome Jesus
and we thank you for all the love
and hope and peace he brings us.
Help us to be like Jesus
and bring love and hope and peace
to each other.
Let the love in our family
reach out to everyone we meet
today and tomorrow and every day.

Prayer after Christmas
Pat Corrick Hinton

Lord,
it's quiet now.
The glitter and the noise,
the excitement and the feasting
are winding down.
In this rest and peace
after the celebration of Christmas,
let us quietly think
of you
and your love
and your peace.
Thank you for coming to us.
Please stay with us always.

Bless Us, Dear God
Christopher Idle

O God our Father,
we pray that you will bless every baby born at Christmastime;
their mothers, their families, their homes.
May they receive a better welcome from our world
than Jesus did;
and may they come to know him
as their Savior and Friend. For his sake. Amen.

A Christmas Prayer

Grant, heavenly Father,
that as we keep the birthday of Jesus,
he may be born again in our hearts,
and that we may grow in the likeness
of the Son of God,
who for our sake was born Son of Man.

O Lord Jesus

O Lord Jesus, who for love of us
lay as a baby in the manger,
we thank you that by your coming
you brought joy to all the world.
Help us at this glad time
to try to make others happy for your sake.

Thank You for Our Christmas Tree
Mildred Tengbom

Dear God, thank you for our Christmas tree,
for the presents we get,
and for the Christmas cookies and goodies.
But thank you most of all for baby Jesus.
Amen.

We Remember Jesus
M. H. Botting's collection

O God, our Father,
as we remember the birth of your Son, Jesus Christ,
we welcome him with gladness as Savior
and pray that there may always be room for him
in our hearts and in our homes,
for his sake. Amen.

We're Happy at Christmas
Ron and Lyn Klug

We're happy at Christmas
because it's your birthday, Jesus.
Thank you for coming to be with us.
Thank you for Christmas trees
and presents and bright lights
and good things to eat.

Let Us Thank God for Christmas
J. D. Searle

Let us thank God for Christmas:
For this happy and exciting time of the year
  Thank you loving Father.
For Christmas trees and decorations
  Thank you loving Father.
For cards and presents and good food
  Thank you loving Father.
For fun with family and friends
  Thank you loving Father.
For singing carols and listening to the Christmas story
  Thank you loving Father.
For all these things because we have them
to remind us of the coming Jesus
  Thank you loving Father.

Christmas Prayer
Robert Louis Stevenson

O God, our loving Father,
help us rightly to remember the birth of Jesus,
that we may share in the song of the angels,
the gladness of the shepherds,
and the worship of the Wise Men.
May the Christmas morning make us happy to be your children
and the Christmas evening bring us to our bed with grateful thoughts,
forgiving and forgiven,
for Jesus' sake. Amen.

Dear Baby Jesus
Margaret Kitson

Dear baby Jesus,
we have come to find you
in the stable at Bethlehem.
May we love you as Mary loved you.
May we serve you as Joseph served you.
May we worship you as the angels worshiped you,
Jesus, our King.

I'm So Excited!
Chris Jones

I'm so excited, Jesus!
Christmas is such a great time—
full of gifts and surprises.
But you were the biggest surprise of all
because no one thought you'd come
as a tiny baby
and be born in a poor place like a stable.
You were the best gift of all, too,
a gift from God to bring us life forever.
Thank you for being the biggest surprise
and the best gift.

Carols

The Friendly Beasts

Robert Davis

Medieval French Carol

1. Je - sus our broth - er, kind and good, was hum - bly born in a
2. "I," said the cow all white and red, "I gave him my man - ger
3. "I," said the dove from the raf-ters high, "Cooed him to sleep that he

sta - ble rude, and the friend - ly beasts a - round him stood;
for his bed, I gave him my hay to pillow his head."
should not cry, We cooed him to sleep, my mate and I."

Je - sus our broth - er, kind and good. "I," said the don - key,
"I," said the cow all white and red. "I," said the sheep with
"I," said the dove from the raf - ters high. Thus ev - 'ry beast by

shag - gy and brown, "I car - ried his moth - er
cur - ly horn, "I gave him my wool for his
some good spell, in the sta - ble dark was

up hill and down; I car - ried his moth - er to
blan - ket warm, he wore my coat on
glad to tell of the gift he gave Em -

Beth - le - hem town." "I," said the don - key shag - gy and brown.
Christ - mas morn." "I," said the sheep with cur - ly horn.
man - u - el, the gift he gave Em - man - u - el.

Away in a Manger

American

American

1. A - way in a man - ger, no crib for his
2. The cat - tle are low - ing; the poor ba - by
3. Be near me, Lord Je - sus; I ask you to

bed, the lit - tle Lord Je - sus laid down his sweet
wakes, but lit - tle Lord Je - sus no cry - ing he
stay close by me for - ev - er and love me, I

head; the stars in the sky____ looked down where he
makes. I love you, Lord Je - sus; look down from the
pray. Bless all the dear chil - dren in your ten - der

lay, the lit - tle Lord Je - sus a - sleep on the hay.
sky and stay by my cra - dle till morn - ing is nigh.
care and fit us for heav - en to live with you there.

Pat-a-Pan

Bernard de la Monnoye

Bernard de la Monnoye

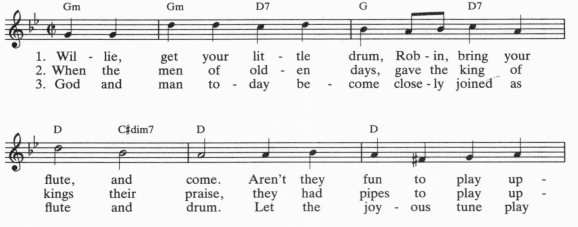

1. Wil - lie, get your lit - tle drum, Rob - in, bring your
2. When the men of old - en days, gave the king of
3. God and man to - day be - come close - ly joined as

flute, and come. Aren't they fun to play up -
kings their praise, they had pipes to play up -
flute and drum. Let the joy - ous tune play

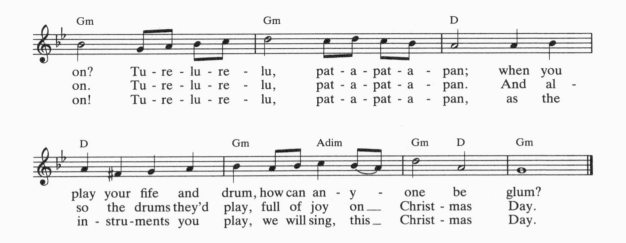

on? Tu - re - lu - re - lu, pat - a - pat - a - pan; when you
on. Tu - re - lu - re - lu, pat - a - pat - a - pan. And al -
on! Tu - re - lu - re - lu, pat - a - pat - a - pan, as the

play your fife and drum, how can an - y - one be glum?
so the drums they'd play, full of joy on __ Christ - mas Day.
in - stru - ments you play, we will sing, this __ Christ - mas Day.

Mary Had a Baby

Traditional Spiritual

Traditional Spiritual

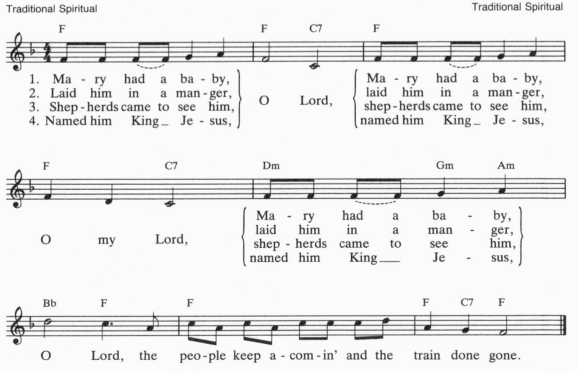

1. Ma - ry had a ba - by,
2. Laid him in a man - ger,
3. Shep - herds came to see him,
4. Named him King __ Je - sus,

O Lord,

Ma - ry had a ba - by,
laid him in a man - ger,
shep - herds came to see him,
named him King __ Je - sus,

O my Lord,

Ma - ry had a ba - by,
laid him in a man - ger,
shep - herds came to see him,
named him King __ Je - sus,

O Lord, the peo - ple keep a - com - in' and the train done gone.

Hush, My Babe, Lie Still and Slumber

Isaac Watts

Kentucky Carol

1. Hush, my babe, lie still and slum - ber,
2. How much bet - ter art thou at - tend - ed
3. Soft and eas - y is thy cra - dle,

ho - ly an - gels guard thy bed, heav'n - ly bless - ings
than the Son of God could be when from heav - en
coarse and hard the Sav - ior lay, when his birth - place

with - out num - ber gent - ly steal - ing on thy head.
he de - scend - ed, and be - came a child like thee.
was a sta - ble, and his soft - est bed was hay.

I Am So Glad Each Christmas Eve

Peter Knudsen

Marie Wexelson

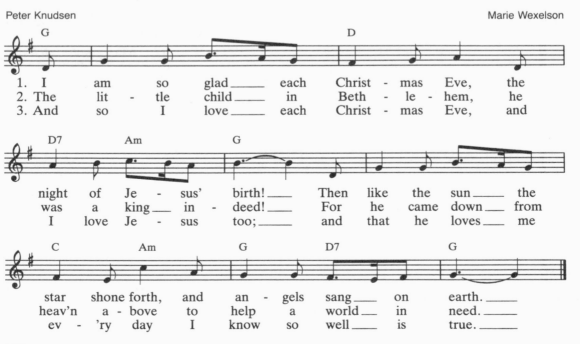

1. I am so glad each Christ - mas Eve, the
2. The lit - tle child in Beth - le - hem, he
3. And so I love each Christ - mas Eve, and

night of Je - sus' birth! Then like the sun the
was a king in - deed! For he came down from
I love Je - sus too; and that he loves me

star shone forth, and an - gels sang on earth.
heav'n a - bove to help a world in need.
ev - 'ry day I know so well is true.

Go Tell It on the Mountain

Refrain, Spiritual
Stanzas, John W. Work Jr.

Spiritual

Refrain

Go tell it on the moun - tain, o - ver the hills and
ev - 'ry - where; go tell it on the moun - tain that
Je - sus Christ _ is born! *Fine*

1. While shep-herds kept their watch-ing o'er
2. The shep-herds feared and trem-bled when,
3. Down in a lone - ly man - ger the

si - lent flocks by night, be - hold, through-out the
lo, a - bove the earth rang out the an - gel
hum - ble Christ was born; and God sent us sal -

to Refrain

heav - ens there shone a ho - ly light. _____
cho - rus that hailed our Sav - ior's birth. _____
va - tion that bless - ed Christ - mas morn. _____

Rise Up, Shepherd, and Follow

Traditional Spiritual   Traditional Spiritual

1. There's a star in the East on ___ Christ - mas morn,⎱
2. If you take good ___ heed to the an - gel's word, ⎰

rise up, shep-herd, and fol - low. ___ ⎰It will lead to the place where the
                                       ⎱You'll for - get your ___ flock, you'll for -

Sav - ior's born; ___⎱ rise up, shep-herd, and fol - low. ___
get your herd; ___⎰

Refrain

Leave your ewes and leave your lambs, rise up, shep-herd, and

fol - low, ___ leave your sheep and leave your rams,

rise up, shep-herd, and fol - low. ___ Fol - low, fol - low,

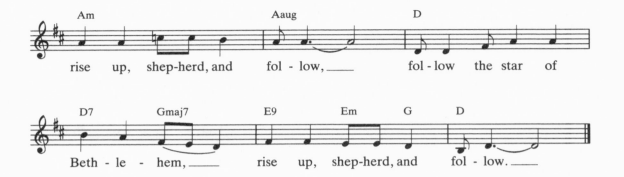

rise up, shep-herd, and fol - low, _____ fol - low the star of

Beth - le - hem, _____ rise up, shep-herd, and fol - low. _____

O Little Town of Bethlehem

Phillip Brooks

Lewis H. Redner

1. O lit - tle town of Beth-le-hem, how still we __ see thee lie! A -
2. For Christ is born of Ma - ry, and gath-ered_ all a - bove, while
3. How si - lent-ly, how si - lent-ly the won-drous_ gift is given! So
4. O ho - ly Child of Beth-le-hem! De - scend to __ us, we pray; cast

bove thy deep and dream-less sleep the si - lent_ stars go by. Yet
mor-tals sleep, the an - gels keep their watch of__ won-d'ring love. O
God im - parts to hu - man hearts the bless-ings_ of his heaven. No
out our sin and en - ter in, be born in__ us to - day. We

in thy dark streets shin - eth the ev - er - last - ing Light; the
morn-ing stars to - geth - er pro - claim the ho - ly birth, and
ear may hear his com - ing, but in this world of sin, where
hear the Christ-mas an - gels the great glad tid - ings tell; O

hopes and fears of all the years are met in thee to - night.
prais - es sing to God the King, and peace to men on earth!
meek souls will re - ceive him still, the dear Christ en - ters in.
come to us, a - bide with us, our Lord Im - man - u - el!

125

We Three Kings of Orient Are

John H. Hopkins

John H. Hopkins

1. We three kings of O - ri - ent are; bear - ing
2. Born a King on Beth - le - hem's plain, gold I
3. Frank - in - cense to of - fer have I, in - cense
4. Myrrh is mine, its bit - ter per - fume breathes a
5. Glo - rious now be - hold him a - rise, King and

gifts, we trav - erse a - far field and foun - tain,
bring, to crown him a - gain, King for - ev - er
owns a De - i - ty nigh. Pray'r and prais - ing
life of gath - er - ing gloom; sor - r'wing, sigh - ing,
God and Sac - ri - fice, Al - le - lu - ia,

moor and moun - tain, fol - low - ing yon - der star.
ceas - ing nev - er o - ver us all to reign.
all men rais - ing, wor - ship him, God most high.
bleed - ing, dy - ing, sealed in the stone cold tomb.
Al - le - lu - ia, earth to the heav'ns re - plies.

Refrain

O____ star of won - der, star of night, star with

roy - al beau - ty bright, west - ward lead - ing still pro -

ceed - ing, guide us to thy per - fect light.

Acknowledgments

Every effort has been made to trace the ownership of all copyrighted material and to secure the permissions necessary to reprint these selections. Any error or oversight will be corrected in future printings if such omission is made known.

The following copyrights are acknowledged:

9   Copyright © 1987 Augsburg Publishing House.

12   Copyright © 1982 *The Church Herald*. Used by permission.

14   Used by permission of Margaret Shauers.

16   Used by permission of Gloria A. Truitt.

18   Used by permission of Betty Lou Mell.

23   Reprinted by permission from *Collected Poems of Sara Teasdale*, copyright © 1937 Macmillan Publishing Co.

24   Used by permission of Gloria A. Truitt.

26   "The Christmas Train" by Ivan Gantschev, translated by Stephen Corrin (Frederick Warne, 1982), copyright © 1982 Bohem Press, Zurich, translation copyright © 1982 Frederick Warne, Ltd. Used by permission.

28   Used by permission of The Frederick Harris Music Co., Ltd.

29   Used by permission of Margaret Springer.

31   Used by permission of Marjorie Ellert Berg.

36   Copyright © 1987 Augsburg Publishing House.

41   Used by permission of Hope Lind.

43   Used by permission of Helen Mallmann.

47   Used by permission of Mable N. McCaw

51   Reprinted from *Animals at the Manger* copyright © 1969 Augsburg Publishing House.

52   Reprinted by permission from *The Story Teller* by Maud Lindsay copyright © Lothrop, Lee, and Shepard.

56   Used by permission of Evelyn S. Wilharm.

58   Reprinted by permission from *Story World* copyright © American Baptist Board of Education and Publication.

61   Copyright © 1987 Augsburg Publishing House.

62   Used by permission of Margaret Shauers.

64   Reprinted from *The Long Christmas* copyright © 1941, 1969 Ruth Sawyer. Used by permission of Viking Penguin, Inc.

65   Used by permission of Kit Lambeth.

69   Used by permission of Margaret Shauers.

70   Reprinted from *All Through the Year: Three Hundred and Sixty-five Poems for Holidays and Everyday* (J. B. Lippincott) copyright © 1932, 1960 Annette Wynne. Used by permission of Harper and Row, Publishers, Inc.

71   Copyright © 1987 Augsburg Publishing House.

74   Used by permission of Mona K. Guldswog.

76   Copyright © 1987 Augsburg Publishing House.

78   "Kurt Finds Christmas." Used by permission of Nelda Johnson Liebig.

80   Used by permission of Alice Sullivan Finlay.

83   Reprinted from the December, 1967 issue of *Hand In Hand* copyright © 1967 Augsburg Publishing House.

85   Used by permission of Marty Crisp.

87   Reprinted by permission from *Merry Christmas Stories* copyright © 1926, 1954 Albert Whitman & Co.

90   Used by permission of Alan Cliburn.

93   Reprinted from *The Collected Poems of G. K. Chesterton*. Used by permission of Dodd, Mead, and Co., Inc.

94   Used by permission of Alice Cameron Bostrom.

95   Used by permission of Celia Lehman.

97   Used by permission of Phyllis Doudna.

98   "Christmas Is Remembering" by Elsie Binns from *Story Parade* copyright 1945 by Story Parade, Inc. Copyright renewed 1973. Reprinted by permission of Western Publishing Company, Inc.

99   Copyright © 1987 Augsburg Publishing House.

101 Reprinted from the December 26, 1956 issue of *Child's Paper* (Wartburg Press) copyright © 1956 Augsburg Publishing House.

103 Reprinted from the January 1951 issue of *Child's Prayer* (Wartburg Press) copyright © 1951 Augsburg Publishing House.

106 "A Bell Cookie." Used by permission of Elizabeth Phillips.

112 Reprinted from *Child's Christmas Chimes* (Lutheran Publishing House) copyright © 1942 Augsburg Publishing House.

114 "Thanks for God." Reprinted from *You Promised, Lord* by Ron Klug copyright © 1983 Augsburg Publishing House.

115 Reprinted by permission from *Prayers After Nine Raining Days and Other Family Prayers* copyright © 1978 Pat Corrick Hinton.

116 "Bless Us, Dear God." Used by permission of Kingsway Publications, Ltd.

116 "A Christmas Prayer" and "O Lord Jesus." Reprinted from *Prayers and Hymns for Junior Schools* copyright © 1933 Oxford University Press.

116 "Thank You for Our Christmas Tree." Reprinted from *Table Prayers* by Mildred Tengbom copyright © 1977 Augsburg Publishing House.